Line of Sight

Line of Sight

The Five Keys for Strategic Execution in an Age of Uncertainty

Robert Courser
& Olivier Aries

Forefront
BOOKS

Published by Forefront Books.
Distributed by Simon & Schuster.

Library of Congress Control Number: 2023918130

Print ISBN: 978-1-63763-214-7
E-book ISBN: 978-1-63763-215-4

Cover Design by Bruce Gore, Gore Studio, Inc.
Interior Design by Bill Kersey, KerseyGraphics

To Kim Courser, my mom; to Dan Courser,
my dad, best friend, and favorite person,
without whom I wouldn't be much! – RC

"If you want to build a ship, don't drum up the
men to gather wood, divide the work, and give
orders. Instead, teach them to yearn for the vast
and endless sea." Antoine de Saint-Exupéry – OA

Contents

CHAPTER 1

The Founder's Trap

Before we explore the practices to escape what I call the Founder's Trap, allow me to introduce myself. My name is Robert Courser. For more than two decades, I have been guiding small- and medium-sized enterprises through the complexities of scaling up. Having worked with hundreds of companies facing similar challenges to yours, I have developed a proven methodology that can effectively unlock your organization's growth potential.

In this book, I will share with you the tools and insights that have enabled my clients to grow successfully. My expertise lies in analytics, applied to both human behavior and operations. As the founder and owner of Synergistics Systems, a behavioral analytics consultancy, and the CEO of Line-of-Sight, the strategy execution platform that gave its name to this book, I leveraged data-driven insights to build my companies, and I am now helping my clients use data to make thoughtful, effective decisions to build and grow their own.

Before I became a growth consultant, I was a culinary expert by trade. I like to draw parallels between the precision required to prepare a meal and the precision needed to build a successful company. With my clients, I emphasize flawless execution, effective leadership, intentional focus, and precise alignment; this approach is inspired by the Japanese concept of *Kappo*. *Kappo* emphasizes capturing the moment when an ingredient is at its freshest, purest state.

My passion for gastronomy led me to attend the School Craft College of Culinary Arts, where I honed my skills and gained valuable experience at several high-end restaurants in my hometown of Ann Arbor, Michigan. Eventually, I became executive sous chef at Opus One, working closely with renowned Chef Tim Gisinski, before moving on to become executive sous chef at Seldom Blues, where I helped the restaurant achieve the prestigious title of Restaurant of the Year under Chef Jerry Nottage.

Over time, I realized that my culinary experience was quite transferable to business: *Kappo* continues to be my North Star when I work with business owners and CEOs. Together, we aim to achieve as perfect an alignment as possible between the many parts that make up their business. We call it execution excellence. Over time, me and my colleagues at Line-of-Sight and I developed a methodology and a platform to consistently deliver this promise. Now our goal is to provide every organization with simple, confidence-inspiring analytics and solutions that build their internal alignment—and get things across the finish line.

In the culinary world, *Kappo* delivers outstanding flavor and an unforgettable dining experience. In business, *Kappo*'s ethos of alignment helps company founders, business owners, and leaders build more value, generate greater wealth for themselves and their employees, support their communities, and achieve the long-term legacy and life balance that make it all worth it.

This is where this book comes in. I have seen so many business owners and executives struggle with injecting new growth in their companies and face what we call the "Founder's Trap". I realized my approach to *Kappo* would be a valuable guide for them—if they followed the right recipe.

What is the Founder's Trap?

You're a successful business leader or entrepreneur who has built or led a solid, mid-market company. You've led your business 80 percent of the way toward the finish line. You've done so despite unprecedented market challenges: global competition, COVID-19, supply chain disruption, an inflation such as we have not seen in decades. Congratulations are in order, and as someone who has advised hundreds of small- and medium-sized businesses (SMBs), my hat is off to you.

Yet there's still a problem. You feel you are not quite able to cross the tape and declare victory. You might be struggling to scale your business. Your employees might be quitting. You might be sitting on too much inventory. Your world is as uncertain as ever. Perhaps, if you own your own business, you are even thinking about selling, but you know you will leave money on the table; your legacy won't be fully realized. You're beginning to

> The Founder's Trap: the recognition that the methods and skills you excelled at to start, grow, and lead your business aren't the same skills required to scale it further.

bump against the Founder's Trap: the recognition that the execution methods you excelled at to start and grow your business aren't the same skills required to scale it further.

Let me assure you that your challenges are not unique. I've witnessed up-close the feelings of frustration and sometimes failure that leaders experience when they think they've hit their own ceiling. To quote Marshall Goldsmith's famous book title: What got you here won't get you there.

The good news is that after we identify the common challenges that other leaders like you are facing, we'll walk together through the best practices to solve them—systematically using objective data. We will discuss the fundamentals of what we call organizational health. Organizational health is a leadership mindset that applies data and discipline to deliver execution excellence.

In this book, we will unpack how you can achieve better organizational health. Just like your own annual check-up, good health starts with measuring your vital signs and examining how your key organs are operating. The same goes for companies: Good health starts with an objective diagnostic, and each aspect of its execution must be examined and addressed to ensure the body's optimum performance.

These key aspects of execution include: a clear mission, vision, and strategic intent; a well-defined market discipline; and five Keys to Strategic Execution, or KSEs: Strategic Understanding, Leadership, Balanced Metrics, Activities & Structure, and Human Capital (Fig. 1.1).

It All Connects

Fig. 1.1. The mission, vision, strategic Intent, market discipline, and the five KSEs work together as a system

The next chapter discusses the importance of a clear purpose to build alignment within the organization, and the outsize importance of people throughout execution. Chapter 3 presents the three fundamental market differentiation options; Chapter 4 to 9 introduce the Five Keys to Strategic Execution; and Chapter 10 is a capstone that allows you to run a self-assessment of your own company's execution capabilities.

We hope this book will give you the ingredients necessary to develop your own flavor of *Kappo*, the near-perfect alignment of capabilities that lets you achieve the growth, performance, and success you're pursuing, however you define your own success.

Purpose And Alignment: The Line-of-Sight Approach

S trategy is a set of guiding principles that, when communicated clearly and adopted widely, provides a basis for decision making across the organization. It's that simple!

Clear Direction and Shared Purpose

Strategy matters (and it matters a lot). But the primary value of a coherent strategy is to be a guide for excellent execution. Yes, a strategic plan is required, but it's not an end in and of itself. It's the necessary first step that you and your executive team envision and initiate. You've done 20 percent of the work by defining your goals, but there's 80 percent more work that needs to get done. This work is to align all the elements of your execution to your goals, across your organization.

This is what we call "line of sight": the seamless alignment of key operational elements to reach your intended strategic objectives. Just as in its literal sense where a clear and unobstructed view is essential to see and reach a target, in business, line of sight ensures that every aspect of your organization is focused and synchronized towards achieving your objectives without ambiguity, obstruction, or distraction. This alignment fosters a unified effort, maximizes the use of your resources, and enhances the probability of hitting your goals.

Think of your strategy as a plan to deliver the goals you've set. In this book, we define the components of strategy as: mission, vision, strategic intent, and the market discipline. We'll review them in details in Chapter 3. After you've defined a well-thought-out mission and the objectives necessary to achieve it, you must clearly communicate them throughout your organization, stratum by stratum, from executives to managers to front-line employees. Then, when you implement your strategic plan, the resulting positive changes will substantively impact every single area of your business. And the good news is that the process can be undertaken efficiently.

Jim Collins's book *Good to Great: Why Some Companies Make the Leap ... and Others Don't* discusses this central concept at length. Great companies succeed because they don't stop until they've surmounted the "last

Wrong Strategy or Poor Execution?

"Nearly 70% of well-formulated strategies failed due to poor execution"
–Harvard Business Review[1]

Fig 2.1. Strategy vs. Execution

six inches" on the path to greatness. Put another way, a coherent strategy leads to excellent execution, impacting employee engagement and customer satisfaction.

In this chapter, we will discuss the paramount importance of keeping people at the center of organizational health. When you develop your strategy, your primary audience is your employees. Execution itself is the sum of all activities and behaviors of your employees. Therefore, the five Keys to Strategic Execution are focused on people, and the measurement of organizational health itself is based on the employees' input, as we'll see in Chapter 3.

In this chapter, we will share customer stories to illustrate the critical importance of placing people at the center of your strategy execution.

When your company lacks a strategy or has a vague one, you cannot have focus. You're simultaneously going in multiple directions, and productivity and profitability suffer. You're confusing your most valuable asset: your employees. You are adding more uncertainty to your system by giving employees a reason to leave you.

> People have an innate need to contribute
> to something larger than themselves.

When everyone at every level of your business—from CxOs to managers to departmental employees—shares a common purpose, the company benefits because the people benefit. When everyone in the organization profits (both materially and psychologically), the customer emerges as the ultimate winner.

Think about it: we all want to leave our offices, factories, or retail operations with the feeling that what we do matters. We take pride and satisfaction in knowing we've made a significant and valuable contribution to the organization. When we feel we've made a difference, we feel that what we did that day was meaningful. That feels really good. And when we feel good, we're excited about coming to work the next day. We're motivated to continue to perform well. These attitudes generate confidence—in ourselves and in the leadership of the company. That confidence inspires people to let their competence shine through and do the right thing—this is execution excellence.

Valuing Employees

When a company prioritizes its people and ensures they feel valued, empowered, and motivated to contribute to the organization, everyone wins. Some time ago, we intervened with the Pennsylvania branch of a nationwide life insurance and financial services firm. This organization had a "sink or swim" approach to money managers, who were hired in large numbers because the churn was very high: little training meant many hires were struggling to hit their targets, resulting in their senior partners taking over their clients, leading to further loss of motivation and trust. However ineffective this approach appeared to be, it was just the way things were done. Increased competition led the management to seek our guidance to improve sales performance. We helped the organization develop a more comprehensive training, create an onboarding process that provided better orientation to new hires, and re-emphasize the central role of individual money managers in the success of the firm through repeated and sustained messaging from the leadership team. None of this was rocket science, but just acknowledging how important people were to the mission of the branch and taking a few visible actions to bolster that position was enough to breathe new life into a badly frayed culture and put the branch back on a healthy growth trend, not least because customers experienced a more stable relationship with their money manager.

The principles we are describing are nothing new; they are universal and timeless, and they're particularly relevant to today's business environment and prevailing attitudes.

According to the Pew Research Center, 35 percent of the current US workforce is comprised of millennial workers born between 1981 and 1996.[2] Maybe more so than others, this generation highly values having a meaningful sense of purpose and accomplishment in their jobs.[3] For them, clarity of direction and focus are paramount.

We drove this point home with a four-hundred employee manufacturer of measuring equipment in the Midwest. The leadership was managing the company with what you might call a traditional, old-fashioned "command and control" philosophy: employees were expected to do what they were told by their managers, with minimal autonomy and even less context for why their actions mattered. Things went well until the employees who had been there since the creation of the company decades ago started to retire. The turnover of new employees hired to replace those "lifers" started to creep until 140 employees left in a single year. That's when we got a call from the leadership team.

It was immediately clear that the issue was the lack of connection of this younger workforce with any sense of company purpose. So we worked with the leaders and the board to dust off the old mission statement, which no one was ever talking about, and refresh it to fit the current market conditions and ambition of the board. We then organized town hall meetings to explain the company mission of all employees. For eighteen months, every single management meeting started with a reminder of the mission and how everyone matters to fulfill it. Within a year, the turnover dropped by 40 percent. We did not ask the leadership team to change their management style; that would have been extremely difficult for them. But articulating their vision better—that was something they could easily do.

We've emerged from the unknowns unleashed by the pandemic. Yet, macro-economic uncertainty persists, and more complexities are emerging in the world, from unstable supply chains to rising economic costs of climate change. We live in a VUCA world (Volatile, Uncertain, Complex, and Ambiguous) that breeds a general state of confusion and anxiety. When people are anxious about the future, they may idealize the past, get stuck in the present, and stymie forward progress. But if your leadership team is clear with employees about your strategy and their role in executing it, anxiety is reduced and positive and productive attitudes prevail.

This helps to create a healthy culture—one with shared objectives and a team mentality—where workers can thrive. There's a relevant adage attributed to Peter Drucker: "Culture eats strategy for breakfast" (Fig. 2.2).

Culture and Strategy

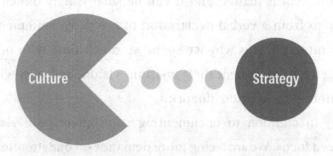

Fig. 2.2. Culture eats strategy for breakfast

Drucker was among the first to affirm that workers place significant value on their workplace's culture, its shared purpose, and its atmosphere. That's the foundation of a healthy business, and that is particularly meaningful for millennials, who value collaboration over competition.[4]

Bridging the Gap Between Strategy and Execution

You can go from strategy to successful execution with a written blueprint, and with focus. Let's start with the written blueprint. You cannot just talk about your vision; it is key to write it down. When you document your intent, everyone in your company is literally on the same page. Memories can fade and people may have different recollections of what was said, but if it is written, there is no room for ambiguity and interpretation. Words matter, and it can be surprisingly difficult to go from a verbal declaration to a written statement of intent. This is why we spend so much time with our clients to document their mission, vision, and strategic intent—the written blueprint.

In addition to documenting your intent, you also need focus. We are facing more demands on our attention than ever before. Our world is more complex and uncertain, with more technologies to master, more risks, and more opportunities. Will I lose my suppliers? How would a recession affect my pricing and my bottom line? How do I find and retain exceptional talent? And if I've been building a company, how do I protect my legacy?

We recently worked with an aerospace company acting as a contractor for the US Department of Defense. The firm had grown opportunistically, adding many different lines of business, such as airplane maintenance, as demand arose alongside its original focus on drone operations. However, none of those activities could get enough resources and management attention to really thrive, and growth slowed to a halt.

We worked with the company founder to determine what his ambition really was. Was it to try and be all things to all people, or was it something else? It turned out that the company had developed a competitive edge in intelligence gathering and processing, an area for which the founder also had passion and expertise. We jointly decided to make it the focus of the company: a one-stop shop to provide actionable intelligence, combining drone operations and sophisticated data analysis.

The shift did not happen overnight: The other activities were profitable and were needed to finance the pivot toward intelligence. But every action was geared toward this new focus. In particular, the company made acquisitions in the area of data processing to expand its technological edge. Other lines of business were progressively shed. We've worked with this company for a while now, and over the past seven years, their revenues in intelligence gathering and processing has grown tenfold, allowing the founder to generate substantial personal wealth by getting further funding from a private equity fund.

There are more areas to explore and risks to control than we have capacity for. Even as accomplished leaders, we face a business landscape in which it's easy to miss the mark on priorities. How do we avoid this pitfall? By narrowing the company's initiatives and focusing tasks and activities of employees to only what is necessary to successfully execute our strategy. Documented goals and focus are what allows us to cut through the fog of uncertainty and get resources aligned around what matters, and only that. Remember *Kappo*, the Japanese cooking approach I applied as a chef? Strategy execution is like *Kappo*: organizing the resources in the best possible way, at the right time, with relentless focus on achieving the wildly successful dish you set your sights on.

Diagnostics and Check-Ups

The principles we apply in our advisory practice help our clients optimize their employees' unique work behaviors and motivations. Using our Line-of-Sight approach and assessment platform, we diagnose the organizational health of our clients' business (how much misalignment is there between strategy/intent and execution/actions), identify the reasons for misalignment within their organization, and guide them to plan and execute correction actions to execution excellence. By offering uniquely tailored prescriptions, we help align business operations and employees and enable the successful execution of the strategy. That's how our clients get results, and that's how you and your company will get results! We like to say that organizational health is what allows you to minimize and eliminate the "execution tax"—the many sources of friction, the misalignments, the redundant tasks, and the overlapped roles that leak value out of your business.

Let us first introduce you to the Line-of-Sight methodology and assessment. Line-of-Sight runs a scan of your entire organization for hidden execution vulnerabilities (the "Organizational Health Scan" that helps determine the execution baseline). It is a short, scientifically validated survey with twenty-nine questions that typically takes only nine minutes to complete. It is simple and quick enough that every employee can complete it online. It is also anonymous, which means you'll get the truth—what employees really think about the environment in which they work.

The assessment has three primary purposes:

- It scans the organization's execution performance in five critical areas that determine successful execution, called Keys to Strategy Execution (KSE): strategic understanding, leadership, metrics, activities and structure, and human capital; it pinpoints areas of strength and good execution, and areas of vulnerability where misalignment between intent and action cause the organization to pay an "execution tax" in the form of redundant tasks, unnecessary work, ineffective processes, or sheer confusion about the company objectives; it also determines an overall Organizational Health Index (see Fig. 2.3). Scores on a scale from 0 to 100 (or 100 percent) measure

Fig. 2.3. KSE scores and aggregate
Organizational Health Index - Example

the degree of alignment within the organization to
execute the strategy.

• It allows the company leadership to take tangible
  action. We run review and decision-making sessions
  with our clients' executive teams to review key
  vulnerabilities revealed in the assessment, develop
  solutions, and chart a course of action to close
  execution gaps and ultimately improve their P&L.

• Used as a pulse check, the assessment is run again
  in all or parts of the organization to see if and
  how actions and efforts yield the expected benefits. Rinse and repeat—you can gauge progress

in real time, assess if your action plan needs to be tweaked, and determine when to move to the next area where you can improve your execution capabilities.

The Line-of-Sight employs a unique approach called Confidence-Based Marking (CBM) to rate the twenty-nine survey items across the five KSE. The CBM approach measures both accuracy and confidence through a single four-point scale. CBM fuses both a person's knowledge of a concept as well as their level of confidence in their knowledge into a more complete and powerful set of responses to each item. As each person responded to the items in the survey, they were asked to make a choice between four possible statements. Each of their responses is then plotted into one of the four quadrants (see Fig. 2.4):

- Aligned: optimal execution; solid decision-making; engaged talent; strong leadership; culture of commitment; strong competitive advantage
- Somewhat aligned: mediocre execution; slow decision-making; confused talent; reluctant leadership; culture of compliance; running in place in the market
- Misaligned: crippled execution; flawed decision-making; cynical workforce; ineffectual

Fig. 2.4. Confidence-Based Marking

leadership; demotivated culture; unstable
market power

- Not sure: inconsistent execution; doubtful decision-making; uneasy or anxious talent; discon-
nected leadership; dissatisfied culture; weak
market power

The Line-of-Sight assessment aggregates individual
employees' perceptions into one consolidated reality: the
reality of how the strategy of the organization is executed.

It automatically generates insights typically examined by the leadership team first, and then is shared with all employees along with a corrective action plan. The assessment results also highlight any gap of perception between how *you* see the organization execute and how *your employees* experience it every day. (Spoiler alert: leaders tend to overestimate the execution capabilities of their businesses.) This objective, unvarnished view of execution capabilities, shared by everyone, allows for the self-inspection, which is, in turn, the basis for self-correction.

The survey results are often surprising. We tend to see a disconnect between what executives, middle managers, and employees consider to be vulnerabilities. The diagnostic also prompts questions that leaders and employees may have never thought about: What's the company's mission? Why do customers buy from you and not your competitors? The assessment elicits "aha" moments and most of the time points to low-hanging, easily achievable opportunities. There are also surprising areas revealed where the company performs better than expected.

Once we identify their business's vulnerabilities, our clients progressively build their own leadership team's capability to engage in the measure-analyze-fix cycle to remedy them. To accomplish this, we bring the leadership team together and, as a group, determine out how to address each vulnerability and prioritize the issue to focus on first. Having data that cuts across the organization, irrespective of functions, silos, fiefdoms (which exist even in the smallest of SMBs), and processes, is a great equalizer: it forces the team to think and act as one, bound by a shared assessment, all leaders collectively accountable for sometimes humbling health scores.

When we do this, we typically concentrate on the easiest fix that will bring the biggest improvement fastest. Then we conduct a monthly scan or "pulse check" to monitor progress and determine next steps—are we ready to move to the next improvement area? This gives us new prescriptions for solving additional problems. Overly complicated solutions should not be implemented, so I apply my philosophy that simple solutions are best.

One vulnerable area we often diagnose is the need to improve communication throughout the company. As we've emphasized, it's all about engaging employees. Communication gaps between leaders and their workforce are relatively easy to diagnose and fix. Is the management regularly walking around and interacting with employees or holding virtual town hall meetings for remote employees? Is there a process to keep employees informed, such as an internal newsletter or regular email updates from the top? Does the onboarding process for new hires clearly communicate the company's strategy? Is the strategy regularly discussed in all-employee meetings?

> It's all about engaging your employees.
> People drive progress.

In our experience, employees tend to be receptive to these check-ups and the resulting changes—often more than their leaders. They feel listened to and empowered. Thirty to sixty days after initially administering the Line-of-Sight assessment, we perform another scan and typically start to see significant improvement. The leadership team then moves their attention to another vulnerability, and we help them stay accountable for continuing to execute whatever practice has been introduced to fix the first issue. This is not about going from challenge to challenge like a butterfly; it is about progressively and thoughtfully aligning different parts of your execution to support your goals, and layering good, sustainable practices that will stick.

Chapter 3 delves deeper into the three options for market differentiation we introduced earlier that, taken together, define the strategy for companies like yours.

They are (1) operational excellence, (2) product or service innovation, and (3) customer intimacy.

I'll also give you the tools and insights to become a decisive fix-it leader who can diagnose areas needing attention and figure out effective prescriptions for improvement. You, too, can become a leader who knows how to execute flawlessly!

This said, Line-of-Sight execution is not for everyone. Leaders need to commit if they want to radically improve the organizational health of their company.

To check if you have the right mindset, answer the three questions in the Line-of-Sight Readiness Checklist below:

Line-of-Sight Readiness Checklist

1. Are you willing to hear the truth?
   ▸ When you use Line-of-Sight execution surveys, your employees speak to you candidly. Are you ready to hear them without judgment?
   ▸ Data is data. Take it all. You can't just focus on what's working and rationalizing away what is not.
   ▸ Truth is opportunity. The more you understand how your business truly operates, the

more you can increase its performance and
your own wealth creation model.

- ▶ Be honest with yourself. When was the
  last time you took action or changed your
  mind based on your employees' ideas or
  feedback? If you can't remember, you may
  want to be mindful of your own potential
  resistance to hearing and accepting other
  perspectives than your own.

2. Are you ready to take action?

- ▶ When you ask your employees about their
  daily challenges with execution, you raise
  the expectation that you'll act on their
  input. It's better not to start than to stop
  mid-way.

3. Are you taking the long view?

- ▶ Improvements will be rapid but not instan-
  taneous. Can you commit to follow up on
  improvements for twelve months or more?
- ▶ Quarterly execution checks are built into
  your organizational health improvement
  plan to make sure you and your team
  remain accountable for it. Can you commit
  to attending them and actively engaging
  in them?

In this chapter we discussed:

1. Strategy is a set of guiding principles that, when communicated clearly and adopted widely, provides a basis for decision-making across the organization.

2. Employees have an innate need to contribute to something meaningful, and a clear strategy creates a shared purpose throughout the organization that fosters engagement and motivation. Strategic clarity also reduces anxiety in the face of uncertainty.

3. When a company prioritizes its people by ensuring they feel valued, empowered, and motivated to contribute to the organization, everyone wins.

4. To bridge the gap between strategy and execution, a written blueprint is essential. By documenting the mission, vision, and strategic intent, the organization ensures everyone is on the same page, and execution can focus on the tasks and activities that matter.

5. The Line-of-Sight methodology relies on an assessment of execution performance in five critical areas that determine successful execution, or Keys to Strategy Execution (KSE): strategic

understanding, leadership, metrics, activities and
structure, and human capital.

6. The Line-of-Sight approach is not for everyone;
the readiness checklist helps identify if you are
ready and able to take advantage of the insights it
provides to improve your execution.

CHAPTER 3

Mission, Vision, Strategic Intent, and Market Discipline

Why do customers buy from you versus the competition?

Is this for your operational excellence? Are they buying from you because they'll receive a consistently well-made product with a combination of low price, ease, speed, and convenience? (Think, Amazon.)

Is this for your innovation? Are they buying from you because they'll get a unique, new, state-of-the-art, cutting-edge product or service? (Think, Tesla.)

Is this for your ability to customize? Are they buying from you because they'll receive a fully tailored product or service that addresses their specific needs and problems? (Think, Dell.)

Your Unique Value Proposition

You can't be all things to all people. Your customers buy from you for *one* primary reason. Either because they value the low price and convenience of your product (thanks to your operational excellence), the amount of innovation that goes into your product (thanks to your innovation capabilities), or the intimacy and knowledge of their needs and habits that you've developed (thanks to your customer intimacy). Who do you want to be and what do you want to sell? The answer to that question defines your unique value proposition.

Your Unique Value Chain

After figuring out why people buy from you and what distinguishes your product and services from others in the marketplace, you must figure out how to deliver on that proposition. Those are the activities that must be accomplished to successfully execute it and deliver; they make up your unique value chain.

As we saw in chapter 2, strategy is the link between your value proposition and your value chain; it provides a basis for making decisions that achieve your desired outcomes.

All too often, when I ask executives what their strategy is, they'll answer "It is to grow!" Growth is not a strategy. It's a goal. It does not tell you *how* you will grow.

Remember, strategy is the link between your unique value proposition and your unique value chain. It is how you will organize your business's activities to deliver on the value proposition that your customers expect from you.

> Your strategy represents the link between your unique value proposition and your value chain.

You must identify the three requirements for a competitive business strategy—why, what, how:

(1) define **why** your customers buy from you and not your competitor (that is, your unique value proposition),

2) define **what** specific activities are necessary to deliver that unique value proposition (that is, your unique value chain), and

(3) define **how** your capabilities will enable your company to deliver on its unique promise (Fig. 3.1).

Your Why (Mission)

The mission is built around the "why"—why your organization exists. It is at the core of what universally drives your company and your employees to make progress. It highlights the impact you are making on the world. The mission serves to:

- Identify why an organization exists.
- Drive alignment of purpose within the company, especially in uncertain times.
- Provide a core basis and standard for the use of company resources.
- Set the tone of the internal operating climate.
- Be the focal point for those who can identify with the company purpose and direction.
- Attract the types of employees who will thrive in the culture and environment.

The mission is summarized in the mission statement. A good mission statement is:

- Simple
- Short—a couple of sentences at most
- Indefinitely relevant
- Measurable
- Resonating with all stakeholders: customers, employees, and shareholders

The Disciplines of Competitive Strategy
The Three Agreements

1

Agreement One
Executives must have an agreement on the fundamental business question, which is: Why do our customers buy from us versus the competition? This is sometimes called a customer value proposition.

Mission (why)

2

Agreement Two
Executives must have an agreement regarding the specific things they must do or the activities they must perform to deliver on the value proposition.

Vision (what)

3

Agreement Three
There must be agreement regarding the unique capabilities (know-how, skills, abilities) that enable the company so it can deliver on the value proposition.

Strategic Intent (how)

Fig. 3.1. The disciplines of competitive strategy

For example, Southwest Airlines' mission statement is "to connect people to what's important in their lives through friendly, reliable, and low-cost air travel."

Your What (Vision)

Your "what" is your vision: it describes what success looks like for your organization in achieving its mission. It is summarized in a vision statement that is

- your company's road map indicating what you want to become by setting a defined direction for growth,
- a description of a clear and inspirational long-term change, and
- a guide to help the organization make decisions that align with its mission and declared set of goals.

A great vision statement:

- Provides a clear picture of what your company intends to achieve
- Looks towards the future
- Is simple and only a few sentences maximum
- Is aspirational
- Is a statement your employees align with and love it
- Applies only to your business

- Aligns with and espouses your core values

For example, Southwest Airlines' vision is "to become the world's most loved, most flown, and most profitable airline."

Your How (Strategic Intent)

The strategic intent describes how you will get there. It serves as the top-line goal that all functional strategies and tactics serve to support. It gives your associates the direction and confidence to make better decisions that are in line with the end game. Because execution is about people, the strategic intent is critical for both you as a leader and for your employees:

- To help the company leadership focus on results: Leaders understand that the desired outcome, not actions, is the true measure of high performance and requires teamwork to achieve results. Strategic intent is the bedrock of collaboration. When experiencing setbacks, leaders use strategic intent to help their people rise to the occasion and never settle.
- To help leadership develop people: Strategic intent is a measure that helps raise the performance bar with every hire and promotion. Leaders use it to recognize exceptional talent, move them to be in the best role, and develop

THREE POSSIBLE STRATEGIES

Fig. 3.2. Three possible strategies

future leaders in a way that directly contributes to the company achieving long-term success.

Your mission, vision, and strategic intent will express themselves in one of three strategies—organizational excellence, product or service innovation, and customer intimacy—throughout your organization (Fig 3.2).

For example, you might base your strategy on innovation, but your billing system reflects excellence in its streamlined efficiency. But again, I repeat, the point is that your go-to-market strategic intent focuses on *one* value proposition. It's what you do, what you do best, and why customers buy from *you*.

Let me take you through examples of what each of these three strategic models looks like. They'll help you figure out what you want to achieve with your organization. Then you're on the way to flawless execution!

Operational Excellence

Think about Southwest Airlines. Their value proposition is to deliver a combination of low price, ease, and simplicity, because their goal is to be as profitable as possible. Their model is well-known yet worth looking at again because it is so well designed:

- They developed the internal mantra of "Wheels Up," which means that if the wheels of the plane are up (it is flying), the company is making money. To maximize aircraft utilization, their value chain activities depend on streamlined capabilities and processes with as little variation as possible; for example, ground operations are optimized to maximize turnaround speed.

- Boarding is simplified: the combination of open seating and assigning passengers to groups before they step inside the plane accelerates the process.

- Southwest encourages direct booking on their proprietary reservation platform to minimize third-party costs, gather more intelligence about its customers, and interface with its other operations systems such as crew scheduling.

- Employees are trained cross-functionally, which provides the company with greater operational flexibility and empowers them to make better-informed decisions that optimize overall value for the company and its customers

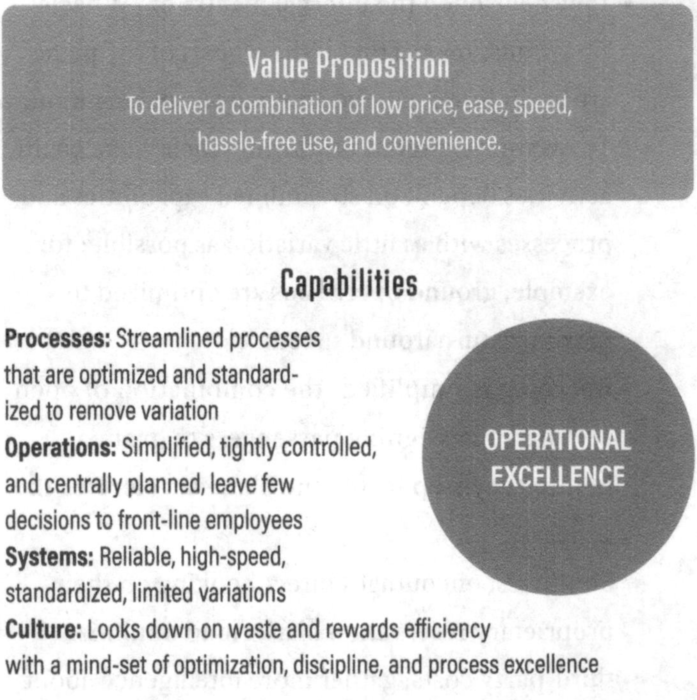

Value Proposition

To deliver a combination of low price, ease, speed, hassle-free use, and convenience.

Capabilities

Processes: Streamlined processes that are optimized and standardized to remove variation

Operations: Simplified, tightly controlled, and centrally planned, leave few decisions to front-line employees

Systems: Reliable, high-speed, standardized, limited variations

OPERATIONAL EXCELLENCE

Culture: Looks down on waste and rewards efficiency with a mind-set of optimization, discipline, and process excellence

Fig. 3.3. Operational Excellence strategy

This strategic model delivers efficiency. Its mindset is one of optimization, discipline, and process excellence (see Fig. 3.3).

As a result of this strategy focused on standardization, Southwest is able to position itself as a low-price, short-haul, city-to-city airline with no business or first-class seating and no in-flight meals. They only fly one type of airplane, the 737. The customer expects this and knows what they're getting every time they fly. Their experience, too, is standardized. Because they offer low prices, repeat business is essential: it is generated by setting and meeting expectations for a no-frills, consistent service. Thus, maybe surprisingly, Southwest's rewards program aimed at building and retaining a loyal customer base is actually an integral part of their operational excellence model.

Southwest shows that operational excellence is a valuable strategy in the service sector, but it is obviously key in manufacturing too—the sector where the pursuit of efficiency was started by Frederick Taylor and later Henry Ford at the turn of the twentieth century.

I worked with a four-hundred-employee, $100 million manufacturing company that sells metal furniture, carts, and racks. Their success has been built on producing a limited range of products with high efficiencies, which allows them to compete against low-cost manufacturers abroad. Maybe more than the other two, this strategy requires relentless focus; indeed it can be tempting to meet the need for more varied products and services at the risk of introducing new complexity. Every couple of years, the salesforce team in this company is advocating for a range expansion to meet the needs of those clients willing to spend more for customized products; but the leadership team knows that more variation in their line-up would diminish their cost advantage and muddy their brand as the US-based, low-price, no-frills provider. Similarly, Southwest stays focused on its model to protect its efficiency advantage, even though demand exists beyond the leisure, budget-conscious, domestic customers it focuses on.

Product or Service Innovation

Think about a medium-sized restaurant of about 250 seats in the Detroit area. This restaurant was one of the pioneers of molecular gastronomy, pushing the limits of the very construct of food—think, ice creams with liquid nitrogen being prepared tableside.

I'm honored to say that I was part of the founding team. From the start, we decided that our business and culinary model would be built entirely on innovation: we accepted high food costs due to the rarity and small purchasing volumes of the ingredients we were using; down to the cooks, the motto was "try it another way" (another version was "let's be weird"); failure was an expected part of success; the high scrap rate (due to the number of experiments that did not produce the absolutely stunning results were always aiming for) was accepted as the cost of doing business. Our menu was priced accordingly, because the value proposition was clear to customers too—they knew that high prices helped fuel our quest to fight the idea that "everything in food has already been done," and they loved being part of that quest.

As a more recognizable brand, Apple still represents the gold standard of original, outside-the-box thinking, which delivers cutting-edge new products. It may appear less so now than it did a few years ago, but this is largely because their brand of innovation has become so ingrained in our consumer culture. The recent release of Apple's Vision Pro mixed-reality headset is proof that the company has not lost its mojo when it comes to developing new products or expanding an existing market with a fresh approach to features, design, or user experience.

Apple's value proposition is still to provide innovative, unique technology products. Apple's operating model is entirely built around innovation:

- They have a functional organization that emphasizes deep expertise in key areas such as hardware, software, design, and marketing. This organization enables them to reach a critical mass of talent and knowledge in each function and let it operate at the leading edge in its field. In turn, this critical mass of expertise is a magnet for talent, which reinforces Apple's technological leadership in a virtuous circle.
- Decision-making tends to be concentrated at the top, which fosters speed and maximizes integration across organizational functions and, therefore, product features. The CEO himself is deeply involved in innovation.
- Design is core to the culture: designers enjoy a special status and play a leading role in product development. With their competitors, engineering is often leading the charge and design is only called in to package new features. At Apple, design leads and engineering follows.
- Apple's investment in research and development is massive: they spent more than $18 billion in R&D in 2020.[5]
- Finally, tight control over product announcements and a practice of secrecy contributes to

> ## Value Proposition
> To deliver innovative, cutting-edge, unique products or services. Customer gets the latest and greatest.

Capabilities

Processes: Focus on invention, product development, and market exploitation.
Operations: Are loosely knit and constantly shifting; entrepreneurial with a desire to work in unexplored territory.
Systems: Measure and reward new product success and don't punish experimentation and risk; allow and support variations that lead to innovation.
Culture: Encourage imagination, out-of-the-box thinking with a mindset driven by the desire to create the future

Fig. 3.4. Innovation strategy

maintaining the aura and mystery of Apple's product development.

Businesses that focus on innovation aren't limited to the technology (or culinary arts) sectors. I consult with a saltwater boat builder that has designed a dual-hull catamaran-style boat for a higher quality ride. Before the company embarked on this innovation, it sold two hundred boats a year. Now it's building a thousand per year. What accounts for that growth? They satisfied an unmet need for a new, more sophisticated product; but they also developed a design that enabled them to build more boats more quickly—another application of innovation. All these examples highlight the value proposition and operating characteristics of an innovation-focused strategy (see Fig. 3.4).

Customer Intimacy

When it comes to customer intimacy, we often think of Disney. They represent the ideal in customer service and intimacy. Disney's value proposition is to provide customized products and services that solve specific problems or address unique customer needs, which they've defined as "making each and every individual customer happy," and the official slogan for the Disneyland theme park is "The Happiest Place on Earth."

For me, customer intimacy is embodied by one of my clients, a Midwest-based manufacturing company producing highly customized surgical solutions. They invest heavily in research and development despite their small size so that they can rapidly prototype and turn around new devices when a particular need emerges.

Just like Disney, my client's processes are flexible, enabling solution development through deep customer relationships and understanding. That's how both companies thrive. Leaders delegate decision-making to employees who work closely with the customer. Employees are intentional in their actions to meet and exceed customer expectations.

A friend of mine recently shared his experience on a Disney cruise with his kids. At 10:30 p.m., he saw a man in what could only have been an executive chef uniform rooting around in the trash. My friend politely asked, "Hi, I'm just curious. What are you doing?" The chef responded that he'd received a report of mushy chocolate-covered strawberries, and he wanted to find some to determine the problem and come up with a solution. Imagine that—the head chef rifling through trash to find a better way to satisfy his guests.

The following morning, my friend received a beautiful array of strawberries delivered to his cabin room with a note saying, "Thank you for expressing an interest in what we do. Enjoy!" This attitude is the epitome of customer intimacy, taking interest in your customers' feedback and then aiming to exceed their expectations. That's how you make customers for life. Figure 3.5 highlights the operating

Value Proposition
To deliver customized and tailored products and services that
solve specific problems or fulfill specific customer needs.

Capabilities

Processes: Are loose and flexible
and enable solution development
through customer relationships
Operations: Delegate decision-
making to employees who work
closely with the customer; very little
red tape to allow for variations

CUSTOMER
INTIMACY

Systems: Geared toward creating
specific results based on customer needs; compensation systems
reward customer retention; enable customer knowledge.
Culture: Embraces continuous improvement and thrives on deep
customer relationships, with a mindset on understanding the customer

Fig. 3.5. Customer Intimacy strategy

elements that allow you to deliver on a customer-centric
strategy.

Working *On* Your Company, Not *In* Your Company

Let's return to your business. Let's say you're a small- to
medium-sized business owner, and you've emerged
nicely from the earlier stages of growth. You've gone from

fifty employees to one hundred fifty, but you can't seem to reach the next level of five hundred employees. You have spurts of growth, but these are followed by slower years, so you never reach your desired outcomes. This means that your business growth isn't scalable or sustainable. What got you here won't get you there. What will? Improving internally.

It's time to start working *on* the business instead of *in* the business. It's time to regroup and evaluate the health of your organization. It's time to revisit your strategy (or conceptualize one if you haven't already) and ensure that you can execute it. Suppose you want customers to buy from you because of your ability to meet their individual needs; in that case, you must examine whether your value chain aligns with your value proposition. Are your employees trained to provide personalized customer service? Are your operations adaptable to new situations?

In the plan you create for your business, there will be elements of operational excellence, product or service innovation, and customer intimacy. But there will be only one primary go-to-market strategy, which removes the most serious impediments to growth. The problem isn't your pricing and it isn't your marketing. And it isn't the fact that your brother-in-law is running the factory. It's the lack of a coherent, easily communicated overall strategy aligning your operations with your intent.

In the next chapter, we'll give you the keys to the kingdom. We'll review the five Keys to Strategic Execution (KSEs) to creating, disseminating, and executing strategy throughout your company. Based on my experience helping hundreds of companies achieve their execution performance and growth goals, I promise these keys will unlock your organization's stagnation. So get ready!

In this chapter we discussed:

1. Strategy is the link between your unique value proposition and your unique value chain. It describes how you will organize your business' activities to deliver on the value proposition that your customers expect from you.

2. You must identify the three requirements for a competitive business strategy: define why your customers buy from you and not your competitor (your mission), define what specific activities are necessary to deliver that unique value proposition (your vision), and define how your capabilities will enable your company to deliver on its unique promise (your strategic intent).

3. There are three possible strategies: *operational excellence* rewards efficiency, standardization, and process excellence; *product or service innovation* emphasizes invention, product development, and market exploitation; and *customer intimacy* leverages deep knowledge of customers and their specific needs.

ONE MORE THING

Additional Perspective on Business Models

The pandemic years forced many businesses to rapidly adapt their strategy to radically shifting market demand, both from consumers and from business buyers. Therefore, it was to be expected that they would pivot toward customer-centric strategies.

To confirm this prediction, we asked 150 CEOs to evaluate how well their organizations were executing their strategies, across a range of industries and company sizes. In particular, we asked them which type of go-to-market strategy they were pursuing (see Fig. 3.6 at the end of this section). You can find more insights from this survey at the end of this book.

The shift in focus to customer-centric business models is clear: 55 percent of CEOs surveyed are now pursuing a customer intimacy–based strategy; companies have had to tune in to rapidly changing demand patterns to adapt all aspects of their execution—sales, customer support, marketing, product development, supply chain, and fulfillment—in addition to moving to a fully or partially remote work environment.

ONE MORE THING

Now that post-pandemic economic growth is here, deep customer intimacy will continue to be a key factor of resilience as the business environment remains unpredictable. McKinsey recently outlined that "both business-to-consumer (B2C) and business-to-business (B2B) companies expect to see meaningful shifts in the shape of future demand."[6] Because of this, McKinsey says, they should continue to maintain a deep understanding of their customer behavior.

If you are the CEO of a company whose strategy is based on customer intimacy, execution will continue to be key. Indeed, CEOs pursuing customer-centric models rate all aspects of their execution consistently high: from strategic understanding, leadership, and balanced metrics, to activities and structure, and human capital. CEOs pursuing alternative strategies tend to acknowledge and tolerate gaps in their execution (for example, companies pursuing operational efficiencies tend to rate the human capital portion of their execution significantly lower than any other dimension).

Here are three good practices that you should consider implementing to stay better attuned to customer demand, especially as an uncertain

ONE MORE THING

economic environment makes customer behavior difficult to predict:

1. Make your strategy clear across your organization.
All your employees need to be aligned on your strategic intent. As CEO, your top role is to make it clear to all. Line-of-Sight's data is unequivocal: CEOs who are unsure about their go-to-market approach rate their own execution performance very low, at least twenty-six points lower than CEOs whose strategy is explicit.

2. Let your customers know they are valued.
Walk the walk on telling your customers that their feedback and input are valued and appreciated. You can do this by appointing customer advisory boards, creating a forum for your customers to communicate, or reaching out to high-value customers and partners before product launches to get their input and ideas. Selectively reach out to customers providing NPS scores to understand in depth what drove their ratings.

3. Over-invest in your human capital.
There is a reason why CEOs pursuing customer intimacy–based strategies rate their execution in the

(ONE MORE THING)

area of human capital 5 points higher than their peers, with a score of 71 versus an average of 68: employee satisfaction drives customer satisfaction and builds the long-lasting relationships that enable intimacy. It was true before the pandemic, and it is even truer now because employees continue to need extra support to heal the mental toll from the crisis.

Fig. 3.6. Strategies pursued at the end of the pandemic

The Five Keys to Execution, and How They Change Everything

In this chapter, we'll talk about the five scientifically validated Keys to Strategic Execution (KSEs) that determine the organizational health of an organization, and why these KSEs are essential to the effective running of your business.

The First Key: Strategic Understanding

Strategy is the backbone of any business operation. Yet, all too often, employees at various levels in the organization do not understand how their company competes and why their customers buy from them instead of the competition.

Strategy must be communicated relentlessly so that everyone in the organization understands their role in making it happen. Defining and communicating strategy is one of the key roles of the leadership team, which brings us to the next key.

The Second Key: Leadership

It all starts at the top. The leadership team are the ultimate decision-makers who shape the business. They are the ones who inspire employees to execute on the company's mission, especially in times of uncertainty.

Inspiration comes from trust. Trust comes from skills and experience (people trust that you are capable), from consistency (you show up as the same person every day), from intimacy (you show genuine interest in others), and from the absence of self-centeredness (you don't make it about you). This means that good leaders tend to be self-aware and be aware of others; they also tend to have strong communication skills and are able to manage change: they know what needs to change, and they can articulate why in ways that resonate with other people.

The Third Key: Balanced Metrics

To put it plainly, this key requires that you measure the right things rightly. Your key performance indicators (KPIs) must provide meaningful data—data that focuses on the requirements for delivering your unique value proposition. Balanced KPIs are a mix of leading and lagging indicators that measure your performance on achieving your strategic mission. Leading indicators are predictive; they look ahead to the future. Lagging indicators look at the recent and current state of your business.

Taken together, these indicators give critical information about your business's progress. But it is not simply a matter of collecting data. When employees are provided with well-defined metrics, they have a clearer understanding of what is expected of them. This clarity helps align their behaviors toward achieving the desired outcomes.

The Fourth Key: Activities and Structure

This key looks at whether the leadership team uses the company's strategy to shape the activities and supporting structures that create the most value for the organization.

Just as the company's strategy and metrics must be meaningful, so must its activities. Additionally, there need to be strong supports in place—procedures, compensation structures, personnel hierarchy, systems, technology, and information flow—that facilitate smooth daily operations.

We recently worked for a company operating a network of locations offering hyperbaric oxygen therapy. This therapy has been cleared by the FDA to treat a number of conditions, including scuba and deep-sea diver decompression injuries (the original application of hyperbaric treatment), carbon monoxide poisoning, diabetic foot ulcers, skin and bone infections, and other disorders.

The company had invested heavily in equipment (the cost of a chamber can exceed half a million dollars) but was struggling to be profitable; in fact, it could not generate enough cash to continue to expand beyond the original six locations. We determined that the issue was a combination of strategic communication and metrics.

The staff was very devoted to the mission of the company, but this devotion expressed itself through a hyperfocus on the patient experience, at the expense of productivity. For example, appointments were scheduled with significant margin before and after the allotted time, to allow patients to arrive early if they could and not to rush them after their session. This focus on patient care was admirable, but it was not substantially adding to the customer experience; in fact, it reduced the throughput of the facilities, thereby reducing the number of slots patients could have booked. And it obviously negatively impacted equipment utilization, hence the low profitability.

We worked with the leadership to increase productivity and asset utilization with three levers: first, the leadership team made clear that higher profitability was a critical goal, as a necessary condition for the company to survive and strive; second, we honored the staff dedication to their mission by framing the drive for higher utilization as an opportunity to offer hyperbaric treatment to more patients than the company could process at the time. Literally, higher productivity would heal more people. The staff readily appreciated the value of the shift.

Third—and this is why I am telling this story here—we made metrics on productivity and utilization visible to all. That way, employees could immediately see the impact of their actions. We supported these actions with other operational decisions, such as adding scheduling staff to each location to more accurately manage scheduling and keep each facility operating at its peak efficiency. The result of these actions was that the care experience continued to be excellent, and the company was able to restart its growth journey; it is now adding an average of three new facilities per quarter to its network.

The Fifth Key: Human Capital

Human capital is your most valuable resource, and alignment here is essential too. Successful recruitment and retention depend on matching the right person to the right role at the right time. But this needs to be taken one step further: it requires leading and treating your employees the right way—the way *they* want to be treated. Leaders must recognize that when you were born affects your attitude about work. Increasingly, millennial and Gen Z workers seek the purpose-driven work and satisfaction we've discussed. Yes, a paycheck is important, but it is not necessarily the individual's sole priority.

The number one reason millennials leave their jobs is that they don't feel that they are growing and developing as individuals. The second most prevalent reason for leaving is that they don't have a clear sense of mission.[7] These roadblocks are easily overcome by providing learning and development opportunities to increase engagement. It is a simple equation: give your talent what they need, and they will give you more value than you had imagined.

The following chapters discuss each key in detail so you can put them into practice and reap the benefits of a healthy organization. Let's jump in with the first key: strategic understanding.

In this chapter we discussed:

1. The five KSE that determine the organizational health connect to each other as an system.

2. Strategic understanding depends on the leadership's ability to define and communicate the organization's goals across the company.

3. Leadership's role in execution is to inspire employees; leaders need to be self-aware and aware of others to build trust and credibility with employees.

4. Carefully selected metrics provide employees with an clear view of what is expected of them, and align behaviors across the organization toward the activities that matter.

5. The structure of the organization and the activities performed by employees must be focused on what directly serves the strategic intent of the company. Tasks that do not directly or indirectly contribute to that intent should be stopped or redirected.

6. Human capital is your most valuable resource. It requires leading and treating employees in the right way—the way they want to be led.

The First Key:
Strategic Understanding

I n our experience helping small- and medium-sized companies to improve their organizational health, more than 30 percent of organizations rank poorly on strategic understanding, which means their employees have a poor understanding of the company goals. Other studies have found that up to 95 percent of employees are unaware of or don't understand their employer's strategic intent.[8]

To address this challenge, the first step, described in chapter 3, is for C-suite executives to ensure that their business strategy creates a market advantage that can achieve their desired outcomes; it expresses itself in your mission, vision, and strategic intent.

The reason most companies rate so poorly in strategic understanding is not that the leadership team hasn't defined a meaningful strategy. Instead, it's because it isn't fully *understood* across every stratum of the organization. This gap reflects a failure in execution, not in planning. Knowing the principles that guide your decision-making is absolutely essential, and you make the next leap forward by ensuring that *everyone* in your organization deeply understands its strategy and their role in achieving it.

Here's a straightforward example of the difference between knowing versus understanding. You may know a complex algebraic formula, a set of facts you've *passively* memorized. But if you *actively* understand the mathematical concept, you can analyze and use it for problem-solving in a variety of contexts. If your employees understand your strategic formula, they're better able to execute it.

Communicating the Message

So how can leaders ensure that their strategy is understood and, thus, executed by all employees? By relentless communication that permeates all levels of the organization (see Fig. 5.1). The advertising concept known as the rule of seven states that people need to hear and/or see something at least seven times before it sinks in (this rule originates from a parenting book from the seventies: *Parent Effectiveness Training*). Research demonstrates that individuals need to see and hear something seven to ten times before truly understanding and internalizing the information. Therefore, repetition and constant reinforcement are necessary.

Strategic Understanding
General Prescriptions
- Based on a compelling North Star
- Relentless internal communication surrounding Vision, Mission, and Strategic Intent
- Focused on understanding of "Why people buy from us versus the competition"
- Formal rhythm and cadence for internal communication (weekly, monthly, quarterly)

Communication Strategies:
- Limit strategic priorities to a handful
- Provide a concise explanation of what a priority means
- Clarify how a priority will be established
- Explain why a priority matters

Fig 5.1. How to communicate to make sure the strategy is well understood

There are many avenues for such communication, including team meetings, group huddles, one-on-one conversations, quarterly state-of-the-company reports, all-hands meetings, newsletters, and even good old posted signs. A multi-pronged communication approach that saturates your company will go a long way toward promoting strategic understanding.

> Repetition and reinforcement are
> crucial practices of communication.

Some of my clients use "challenge coins" to reinforce their messaging. The military initially developed these small coins or medallions to promote pride and engagement and to reward hard work and excellence.[9] They're inexpensive and can be custom-made with your company's logo and message. These coins can serve as a useful motivational tool in business.

Sharp focus and clear communication lead to greater understanding, motivation, and performance excellence. Thus, misalignment can be prevented or remedied as necessary. According to Gallup, "Providing clarity is everything and can make or break the difference between engaged and not-engaged employees."[10] Sadly, the measure of employee engagement—whether a worker is motivated and enthusiastically committed to their job—is at an all-time low in the United States.

Again, the statistics are dramatic: only 32 percent of the workforce report active engagement, and 17 percent are actively disengaged.[11] The latter group is particularly toxic to an organization, as their performance is poor and they tend to spread discontent. In contrast, actively engaged employees lead to tighter alignment around their efforts to achieve desired outcomes. And they feel that they are part of a team with a common purpose, not an anonymous automaton in an assembly line.

Here's an example. A medium-sized manufacturer of high-end aftermarket performance parts for the car enthusiast was struggling with inconsistent quality in the plant that produces custom carbon fiber parts for sports cars. The executive team was relatively new; however, they developed a well-thought-out strategy that turned out to be the company's best kept secret.

Until then, all the employees had heard was "how many parts per week." This led to inconsistent quality on fit and finish, as employees were solely focusing on quantity. After discussing the results and reviewing the data, a town hall was called. The leadership team addressed the issue of "why our customers buy from us versus our competitors." Competitors' products were bought and installed side by side to demonstrate fit and finish to the employees. This led to a much deeper understanding of their own competitive advantage, and this understanding led to a sense of pride in the product.

This message of high-level craftsmanship was continually reinforced through a newly developed internal communications plan that provided weekly communication to every employee in the company with important updates. As a result, quality issues were minimized, customer satisfaction scores improved, and market share increased.

Noticing Your Employees' Efforts in Executing Your Strategy

Another case, that of Paul O'Neill, is an instructive example of how a business leader can develop a simple and powerful strategic intent and communicate it relentlessly to raise employee satisfaction and increase productivity. In 1987, O'Neill became chairman and CEO of industrial giant Alcoa. His first speech to the shareholders and his subsequent execution of a single-minded initiative made him a symbol of industrial occupational safety and health. Alcoa had an abysmal record of worker injuries and accidents when O'Neill took over. He had a laser-sharp focus on safety, a message he constantly hammered away at.

One of O'Neill's solutions was to improve lighting in Alcoa plants. In so doing, worker safety dramatically improved, and productivity and profitability skyrocketed. Subsequent studies revealed that, although improved lighting was a factor in these changes, it wasn't their primary cause. Employee behavior had changed! Workers became more engaged because they felt their needs were being addressed. They appreciated that management cared enough to take action to ensure their safety. This effect is known as the Hawthorne Effect, whereby people's behavior changes when they know (or think they know) they're being noticed. Of course, O'Neill's ultimate goal was to raise profitability, and he was widely successful: Alcoa's net revenues grew from $200 million to $1.5 billion between 1986 and 2000. His single, relentless message on safety was successful in changing attitudes.

It's a misconception that the golden rule (treat others the way you want to be treated) is the best way of engaging and leading people in the business world. Instead, we encourage our clients to apply the "platinum rule," which says that leaders should treat employees the way *the employees* want to be treated. When your employees feel valued and engaged, you receive more of their discretionary mindshare. To be able to apply the platinum rule, you need to take a genuine interest in others and have a way to understand what matters to them and what their needs here. We'll discuss later what data you can use to gain this understanding.

Having the Right People in the Right Roles

Another way to build greater employee engagement is to ensure that you have the right people in the right seats. For example, you may promote a high-performing salesperson to sales manager. This turns out to be a poor business decision. The individual has deep product knowledge and the ability to sell, but a manager's behavioral requirements differ from those of a salesperson; the promoted employee was not psychologically wired to manage subordinates. This promotion was a misalignment between the individual and their role. With the sales manager's—or any employee's—struggles in a role come dissatisfaction and disengagement. We'll discuss this in more depth in chapter 9.

Leaders should apply the platinum rule with all employees—showing genuine attention to others is one of the drivers for trust, as we've seen. However, it can also be useful to follow the Pareto Principle for guidance on how to prioritize resources, including leaders' focus and attention to their employees (the Pareto Principle, better known as the 80/20 rule, is named after Vilfredo Pareto, an Italian engineer and economist; the idea is that you derive the biggest benefit from shining a laser focus on the vital few, not the trivial many).

In terms of human capital, if you identify your most important relationships and highlight the 20 percent of employees who have the biggest influence on your performance, you can decide to invest a bigger share of your time, energy, and resources into these employees. Of course, you want to treat all your employees with respect and attention; how well you treat everyone will largely determine how much trust there is in your organization. At the same time, you're prioritizing the relationships that matter most to achieve the best results possible.[12] You might do this in particular if some of your top employees are a "flight risk" and you are willing to bump their compensation beyond their peers' to retain them (acknowledging that financial rewards are only one of the many aspects that determine retention).

Remember the platinum rule: Treat others
the way they want to be treated.

To achieve superlative execution, diversity in leadership teams requires more than hiring people with different backgrounds. It also requires a complement of skills ranging from methodical process-oriented individuals to extreme multitaskers who thrive under pressure. This diversity helps solve the "founder's trap" problem by addressing the fact that the skills it took to build a business are not the same as those needed to accelerate its growth.

This requires your leadership team to meet regularly to revisit and clarify the company's strategic intent and to measure its progress. Armed with the results, you're able to put together a communication strategy that targets your weaknesses. This process typically takes between thirty to ninety days. Afterward, we see a dramatic lift in strategic understanding, a jump from 68 percent to 100 percent!

As a leader, you must continually work *on* your company, not *in* your company, because an environment of self-inspection leads to self-correction. When everyone in the organization understands its strategy *and* their role in achieving it, your company moves closer to reaching its unique finish line.

In this chapter we discussed:

1. More than 30 percent of companies rank poorly on strategic understanding; 95 percent of employees are unaware of or don't understand their employer's strategic intent.

2. Communication that permeates all levels of the organization is necessary to ensure that the strategy is well understood; repetition and reinforcement are crucial.

3. Having the right people in the right seat is critical to deliver productivity and employee engagement, and to align behaviors with your strategy.

4. Employee engagement is related to many performance outcomes, and actively engaged employees lead to tighter alignment around their efforts to achieve desired outcomes.

5. While you should treat all employees with respect and attention, you should also focus on the 20 percent of your employees who have an outsized impact on your company's performance.

ONE MORE THING

An Additional Perspective on Strategy

Do you know what the two numbers are that summarize the plight of most leaders? It is 90 percent and 95 percent.

In 2005, famed Harvard researchers Robert Kaplan and David Norton published a groundbreaking article on business strategy. The opening salvo of their research was a sobering number: out of nearly two thousand large corporations around the world, our first number (90 percent) failed to achieve their strategic targets. Worse, the vast majority failed to achieve profitable growth—they did not grow enough to earn their cost of capital.

You may think that the state of business has improved since then. It has not.

In 2013, McKinsey & Company considered how companies generate economic profit. The landscape it revealed was as dire as when Kaplan and Norton published their paper. McKinsey found that 60 percent of companies in the "big middle" of the economic profit curve generated very little profit: only $29 billion. Most of the profit was created by the

(ONE MORE THING)

20 percent of companies in the top quintile: a whopping $677 billion, seventy times more than the middle. The bottom 20 percent of companies were *destroying* a staggering $411 billion of profit.

The Fastest Way to Destroy Value

Why do the vast majority of companies fail to meet their goals and grow? That is where the second number comes in. Kaplan and Norton found that the single biggest factor to determine whether the strategy will be successful is obvious: *the entire company must be aware of the strategy.*

In their own words, "If the employees who are closest to customers and who operate processes that create value are unaware of the strategy, they surely cannot help the organization implement it effectively."

Their research revealed that 95 percent of a company's employees were unaware of, or did not understand, its strategy.

Here, too, the number has barely budged since their article. In fact, the Predictive Index's CEO survey showed that in 2022 fewer than one in two companies had a business strategy to start with. The number has steadily eroded: it was 66 percent in 2020

┌─ **ONE MORE THING** ─┐

and 76 percent in 2021, when the pandemic forced companies to be surgically focused on survival and adaptation strategies.

The absence of strategy in most companies means that employees are left to their own devices when it comes to figuring out on which basis to make key decisions.

How Do You Become a Member of the Club?

…The elite club of companies that achieve their objectives and create more value than they consume, that is.

The antidote to destroying value is simple. As Kaplan and Norton summarize with simplicity: "The goal is to make strategy everyone's job."

In small- and medium-sized businesses, that means taking simple actions:

- Documenting the strategy you are pursuing; if that strategy is in the head of the founder or the CEO, it is just a matter of writing it down and setting clearly stated objectives.
- Communicating this strategy to everyone, often: setting up town halls to share it formally and providing regular updates at every opportunity.

---(**ONE MORE THING**)---

- As leaders, practicing "management by wandering around" to catch employees "in the act of doing something good" to reinforce the good behaviors in real time and being available to employees who have questions or suggestions about the strategy.
- Focusing dashboards and metrics on the outcomes that measure your execution.
- Training and developing your people to give them the tools they need to successfully perform the tasks that make the strategy happen.

Your Organization's Health Index Evaluation: Strategic Understanding

Use this rating scale to assess the execution capabilities of your organization in the table below:

A: Aligned (4 points)
S: Somewhat Aligned (2 points)

M: Misaligned (-1 point)
N: Not Sure (0 points)

Index	Strategic Understanding Health Assessment Criteria	Your Assessment (A, S, M, N)	Your Score (4, 2, -1, 0 point)
SU1	I have a good understanding of my company's strategy or game plan.		
SU2	My immediate team has a good understanding of our company's strategy or game plan.		
SU3	In our company, most employees have a good understanding of the strategy or game plan.		
SU4	Most leaders at our company feel it's important for employees to have an understanding of the company's strategy.		
SU5	Our strategy has a practical impact on our performance by guiding our work on a day-to-day basis.		
SU6	Members of my immediate team feel a greater sense of purpose when we understand the business strategy and how our work contributes to it.		
SU7	Members of my team know who our main competitors are and how we differentiate from our competition.		

Total Score _____

From a strategic-understanding standpoint, the health of your organization is as follows:

- If your total score is 14 or less, your organization is not feeling well.
- If your score is between 14 and 24, your organization is going about its day but is not able to run a sprint without feeling depleted.
- If your score is 25 or above, your organization is very fit. It can tackle any challenge that the world throws at it.

Strategic Understanding prescriptions if your health score is 24 or below:

Develop the Strategy

- Document the organization's goals and objectives, even in simple terms.
- Be as specific as possible; consider using the SMART approach to make sure your objectives are:
  - ► Specific
  - ► Measurable
  - ► Achievable
  - ► Realistic
  - ► Timely
- Keep the number of goals as small as possible, and if achievable, summarize the strategy with one single, paramount

objective. The simpler the strategy, the more memorable it will be for employees and the more actionable and practical it will be.

- Be explicit about the opportunities and goals you are *not* pursuing; strategy is about saying no, as Michael Porter famously said (Fig. 5.3), and employees need to understand which areas and opportunities they should not pursue themselves.
- Explain the rationale behind the goals and objectives. Some executives and employees may not agree with the strategy, but they will likely still commit to it if they understand your thinking process.

Communicate the Strategy

- Repetition is key: take every opportunity to talk about the strategy. It will help employees memorize and internalize it. Consider:
    - ▶ Starting all executive meetings and company-wide all-hands with a brief reminder of the strategy.
    - ▶ Schedule brown-bag meetings to informally discuss the strategy with employees and answer their questions.
- Quote strategic objectives from memory—model the behavior you want your employees to follow.

Be a Role Model for Your Strategy

- Make your decisions based on strategy.
- If you are tempted to make a decision at odds with the strategy, you need to stay disciplined or the strategy needs to be revised.
- Make the decisions you are making visible to show that they are informed by the strategy; discuss your decisions with your team and with your employees to show how the strategy guides your actions.
- When making decisions, explain your rationale so that employees understand the implications of the strategy in their own actions.

Use Executives and Managers as Relays

- Brief your executives and managers before communicating the strategy to all employees.
- Make sure they can answer questions from employees as well as you would yourself.
- Ensure that your organization's leaders understand the rationale behind the strategy:
  - ▶ Create an environment where there is enough psychological safety that executives and managers can ask questions and voice their concerns; most likely, they are also reflecting employees' own questions and doubts.

- ▸ Explain your rationale.
- ▸ They may ultimately disagree with the strategy but you're seeking their commitment nonetheless (you want them to "disagree and commit").

Practice "Management by Walking Around"

- Adapt your work routine to make time to meet with your employees, formally and informally.
- Quiz them gently on their work and on the strategy; query them on how the strategy helps them do their work better and make decisions.
- Give them opportunities to ask questions, and make sure you make them feel comfortable doing so (they need to feel they won't be ridiculed or sanctioned).

CHAPTER 6

The Second Key: Leadership

What makes a great leader? For me, it's about *how to lead a business beyond the initial limitations that hold it back from greatness.* It is about understanding what these limitations are, having the right data to remove these limitations and get unstuck, and taking action on insights to grow, and thrive. In the previous chapter, you read how strategic understanding can be broken down into easily digestible, practical concepts and methods. Here, we'll discuss the simple ingredients that enable leaders to steer companies toward making their strategic vision a reality. Leading means guiding members of an organization toward this achievement. The question is: *How* does a leader inspire employees to execute the company's vision?

It comes down to three main requirements: (1) credibility, (2) communication, and (3) change management. Let's look at each one in depth.

Credibility

We all know people who say one thing and do another. Or who say something so vague or confusing that the message is incomprehensible. Or who make promises and never deliver results. These individuals do not inspire trust or motivate others. Leaders who follow through on 100 percent of their promises 100 percent of the time do. Their communication is transparent. They have integrity (doing what they said they were going to do) and authenticity (their words and their thoughts are the same).

> Good leaders don't duck difficult conversations.

Not only do they share information, but they do so honestly. And they're consistent in what they say and what

Leadership

General Prescriptions

- Do what you say you will do 100 percent of the time.
- Hold employees accountable: How much? Of what? By when?
- Relentlessly pursue effective company-wide communication.
- Develop and invest in your people and **yourself**.

Methods of developing leadership credibility:

- Deliver results
- Remain transparent
- Don't duck tough decisions
- Show consistency in behavior
- Lead by example

Fig 6.1. Prescriptions to build credibility

they do. By leveraging data objectively, they enhance their trustworthiness (see Fig. 6.1).

We've all heard that executives lead by example. But what does that really mean? Their behavior is such that employees try to emulate it, whether consciously or unconsciously. This "shadow the leader" principle operates across industries. It's how we effect change and how we develop people. We've all been to a restaurant where a new server stands slightly behind an experienced worker to learn how to perform their role. We trust the experienced server to do the job well; therefore, the trainee will succeed too.

Credibility is the result of aligned leadership. Employees who sense misalignment or mixed messages at the top will justifiably question the strategy. This, in turn, leads to poor execution. I personally witnessed the following situation: An executive team met to discuss the implementation timeline of a project, and everyone present seemingly agreed to it. At one point, the CEO briefly stepped out of the room and another executive started to vehemently criticize the plan and expressed their intention to push back. Yet, when the CEO rejoined the group, the critic, having possibly thought better of it, did not speak up. It was only after the meeting ended that other participants voiced that executive's concerns with the CEO, and did so sensibly.

In relaying these misgivings, they were not trying to get their colleague in trouble. They were being transparent with the CEO by disclosing dissent. It was an honest effort to achieve alignment. Everyone in the organization needs to hold themselves and others accountable.

There are also instances when the leadership gets into nasty debates. Lively discussion is one thing, but screaming, backstabbing, and using epithets are other things entirely. Think about the effect a heated closed-door argument has on the employees who overhear it. It's okay to disagree, but when a decision has been made, total alignment is necessary to execute it. Disagree and commit. In some cases, it might be preferable for the organization to part ways with an intransigent executive who still won't commit after several rounds of discussion.

Remember that your behavior affects your interactions and impacts others. That's the central tenet of self-awareness. Bruce Lee articulated this truism: "To know oneself is to study oneself in action with another person."[10]

Communication

We repeatedly discuss communication throughout this book. This is because repetition is key in communication! It's necessary to communicate the organization's unique value proposition relentlessly. Why do customers buy from us versus the competition? What do we do? How do we do it better than anyone else? What is our functional strategy? What is your role in the process?

Great leaders communicate regularly, clearly, and actionably. They yield engaged talent who are committed to excellence and to fulfilling the company's mission. A demotivated workforce contributes to an organization's lack of focus, missed opportunities, and possibly, loss of market share. Where there's muck, there's money. The potential to increase revenues is submerged in the mud of sticky, opaque communication.

In addition to communicating the company's strategy, an executive must explain the thinking behind it—the why. Leaders should also actively engage with employees to discuss their strategy—not just to explain the why, but to invite questions and pushback. They should cultivate an environment where employees feel free to question and challenge their leaders to perform better. Therefore, "disagree and commit" should be a value held among the executive team but also among employees. Employees buy into a well-articulated goal and the steps to get there. They understand its value and choose to contribute. And superlative execution comes from everyone's ability to understand and feel that what they do matters, even if they don't fully agree with it.

Since there are many different learning styles, it's helpful to communicate your company's strategy in various modalities. You can discuss it in town hall meetings, set up "lunch and learn" sessions to engage employees in a more casual setting, or remind employees of it every time you walk the manufacturing floor, visit a store, or meet with an employee team in a local office. Obviously, the message needs to cascade from the top down: as the business owner or the CEO, you should not be the only one talking strategy; the same principles of credibility and communication apply to leaders at every stratum of an organization, not just the C-suite. Frontline managers may be even better equipped to openly communicate with their team members. So make sure to regularly meet with your managers and explicitly ask them to be your relays across the organization.

Change Management

By definition, getting a company unstuck requires change. And most human beings are uncomfortable with change and are risk-averse. When an employee is asked to work in an different environment, or to perform their work differently, they might infer that their performance is poor and their work isn't valued; or they might be worried because they don't know what their work and their future will look like. Then impending change becomes a traumatic situation, not a positive adjustment, and employees may dread or resist the change.

How do effective leaders mitigate and overcome this resistance? They manage change by communicating over and over, by continuously reminding employees why change is necessary, by explaining what everyone stands to gain if change succeeds, by moving at the pace of the organization and its behavioral culture, and by engaging employees in the design of the change itself. Sustainable change happens over time. Leaders may have spent months identifying strategic improvements; once they're greenlighted, they're understandably anxious to pivot in the new direction.

Sometimes, however, it's necessary to slow down before you speed up. You'll get better results if you communicate to workers *what* the plan is before jumping in. And you'll get smoother execution if you communicate *why* you're jumping in.

An ancient Chinese proverb offers this wisdom: "When the student is ready, the teacher will appear." Willing acceptance of change depends on timing. Lao Tzu continues: "When the student is truly ready, the teacher will disappear." Once a worker has incorporated the leadership's methods, they'll be able to implement them independently. The ultimate result is that the change happens. Your desired outcomes are successfully executed!

The behavioral traits of manufacturing employees and the nature of their work can present an significant roadblock to change; the same goes for employees in positions that require steadiness and structure, attention to details, and consistency. On the manufacturing shop floor (or in, say, an accounting team), the employees' responsibilities require patience, structure, repetition, and precision.

Leaders must appreciate these attributes (which are often different from their own) and communicate and organize the work accordingly to achieve their desired outcomes.

Here is an example of the need to appreciate how people's behaviors and the nature of their work can determine internal processes. A large manufacturer of surgical and medical equipment was struggling to grow and be profitable. When we intervened and conducted our execution assessment, we realized that their product development process was the issue: every time the R&D team developed a new device, the company struggled to scale it into production. This was causing delivery delays and customer frustration, and an uptick in employee turnover. It turned out that manufacturing engineers felt rushed and not given enough time to work out the kinks of new production lines. To solve this issue, we re-engineered the rollout process to nestle manufacturing teams within product development at an earlier stage, giving them more time to design, set up, test and ramp up manufacturing lines. This mitigated the risks associated with new medical device launches, resulting in a shortened time frame from research and development to customer fulfillment, greater customer satisfaction, and a better work environment, especially well-suited for manufacturing employees.

In this chapter we discussed:

1. To make strategic intent a reality, the three main requirements for leadership are credibility, communication, and ability to lead change management.

2. Credibility is built through leadership alignment (i.e. the leadership team speaks with one voice), transparency, consistency, and accountability. Executives must lead by example and ensure total alignment after a decision has been made—if necessary, by following the "disagree and commit" approach.

3. Communicate the organization's unique value proposition relentlessly. Good leaders communicate regularly, clearly, and actionably, and should explain the thinking behind their strategy to engage employees in understanding the company's mission.

4. Employees should feel free to question and challenge their leaders.

5. To guide the company through change, leaders must understand the behavioral makeup of the employees and adapt the work organization, communication, and pace accordingly.

ONE MORE THING

An Additional Perspective on Leadership

A few months ago, we organized a roundtable for senior executives on the topic of "strategic and operational frameworks post-Covid." We were expecting to hear about increased digital delivery, sustainable supply chains, changing customer behaviors, and continued uncertainty. But something interesting happened: all that those leaders wanted to discuss was leadership and people. That was the only perspective that mattered to them when considering their strategies and operations.

Behind Execution, People

As one of these executives put it: "nimbleness in the extreme: it has served the organization well, but it's exhausting for our staff."

Execution, especially when a crisis calls for rapid adaptation, is all about people. Quickly pivoting to a new strategy? It's on the employees. Finding creative ways to operate despite shortages? It's on the employees. Staying focused on what matters despite uncertainty? It's on the employees.

(ONE MORE THING)

Of course, leaders still need to lead from the front, constantly clarifying, explaining, and role-modeling the strategy. But when it comes to executing the strategy, those who know what's going on are the employees.

This is why, over the past two years, we have been by the side of SMB owners and CEOs to rapidly assess and improve their execution capabilities. And we have done that by surveying those who really know: their employees.

Strategy Perception is Execution Reality

When CEOs seek our help to improve their performance, we use the Line-of-Sight platform to assess the execution health of their company. Typically, they come to us because something is not right: perhaps their production runs have shortened in the pandemic, wreaking havoc with their manufacturing shifts; or their middle management has become cynical and lost trust in leadership; or the company has been pursuing two very different segments and is struggling to fulfill them with different operating models.

Regardless of the issue, our first step is to baseline their execution capabilities. We do this by surveying

(ONE MORE THING)

their employees, the people who have the most intimate knowledge of what it takes to deliver, day in and day out.

It may seem counterintuitive to survey employees; after all, isn't the leadership better aware of the company strategy?

Well, that is the point. Every day, employees will behave and make decisions based on what *they* think the strategy is. Their *perception* of what the company is trying to do becomes the *reality* of how things get done.

The Five Keys to Strategic Execution

So, if an executive wants to know how well they are executing and where issues are, we go straight to employees and measure the organization's capabilities based on employees' input in five areas:

1. How is the leadership perceived to lead execution?
2. How relevant are metrics for guiding people in their daily decisions?
3. How related are daily activities to the strategy, and how does the structure make it easy to perform them?

┌─────────────────────────────────────┐
│   **ONE MORE THING**   │

4. How well is talent recruited and developed to directly support the strategy?

5. What do they think is the reason customers buy from their company?

Of course, you know that these dimensions are the five Keys to Strategic Execution (KSEs). They can be scored based on aggregate ratings provided by employee responses. A score of 80 to 100 indicates strong capabilities; a score of 40 or less requires immediate attention from the leadership.

Ask and You Shall Receive

The value of using employees' input to assess how they execute the strategy should not come as a surprise. For years, companies have conducted engagement surveys to understand how employees feel about their workplace. Engagement has a direct impact over individual productivity and collective performance.

Similarly, the sum of individual employee actions determines the collective execution of the organization, and therefore its performance. So it is worth asking the employees for their individual perspective
└─────────────────────────────────────┘

┌─ **ONE MORE THING** ─┐

on what guides their actions and what supports or hinders them.

It's on the Leaders

Once employees' responses have helped build the execution baseline, it's on their leaders to hear the message and act. To help drive the point, we always ask executives to also self-assess their organization's execution capabilities, separately from their employees. In most cases, leaders overevaluate the execution health of their organization; their scores are materially higher than those provided by their employees. This exercise is useful to help them realize they should not trust their own instinct when it comes to execution; they need an objective fact base, which is the aggregate, daily experience of their employees in charge of executing the strategy.

After all, the executives of our roundtable were right: it is really about leadership and people, even when you consider strategy execution.

Your Organization's Health Index Evaluation: Leadership

Use this rating scale to assess the execution capabilities of your organization in the table below:

A: Aligned (6 points)   M: Misaligned (-1 point)

S: Somewhat Aligned (2 points)   N: Not Sure (0 points)

Index	Leadership Health Assessment Criteria	Your Assessment (A, S, M, N)	Your Score (6, 2, -1, 0 point)
L1	The leadership in our company has sufficient credibility with employees to lead the execution of strategy.		
L2	The leadership in our company helps to prepare and move employees through change as needed.		
L3	Our company's leaders continually communicate our strategy in a clear, meaningful, and actionable way.		

Total Score _____

From a leadership standpoint, the health of your organization is as follows:

- If your total score is 9 or less, your organization is not feeling well.
- If your score is between 9 and 15, your organization is going about its day but is not able to run a sprint without feeling depleted.

- If your score is 15 or above, your organization is very fit. It can tackle any challenge that the world throws at it.

Leadership Prescriptions If Your Health Score Is 15 or Below

Maintain a High Degree of Awareness

- Build or reinforce your self-awareness by using behavioral analytics tools such as the Predictive Index:
    - ▶ Know your behavioral drives and how they translate in strengths and areas of caution for your leadership role.
    - ▶ Be mindful of how your behavior may be perceived by others.
    - ▶ Understand and anticipate your "threat rigidity," i.e. how stress modifies your behavior and may lead you to adopt counterproductive attitudes.
- Expand your awareness of others by understanding their own needs and how these needs determine their behavior.
- Follow the "platinum rule" to adapt your own behavior to people's needs and keep them in their zone of optimal performance.

Build and Maintain Trust

- Use the "Trust Equation" to build trust and credibility:
    - ▶ Maintain and expand your technical proficiency by being familiar with all aspects of the business; ask

questions and show interest in the aspects of operations you may have less knowledge of.

▸ Be a reliable leader: show up as the same person every day; be predictable; say what you do and do what you say.

▸ Build intimacy by showing interest in others and their work; ask questions; use behavioral analytics to understand and meet their needs from a behavioral standpoint.

▸ Don't make it about yourself: be authentic but use judgment in sharing information about you, your decisions, your emotions, and your personal life.

Manage Risks

- Understand the key risks that may threaten your strategy and its execution.

- Be mindful of how your behavioral profile and that of your leadership team impacts your organization's and your own risk appetite, and your ability to properly manage risks.

- Be mindful of your own bias (e.g., lack of technical knowledge may lead you to underestimate risks in some areas) and seek the technical advice of relevant employees to form an accurate picture of the risks.

- Treat risks seriously and discuss them with the entire organization at regular intervals; initiate action to make sure adequate risk avoidance and mitigation measures are in place.
- Encourage employees to report risks they see in their respective areas.

Maintain Psychological Safety

- Behave in a way that ensures employees are comfortable sharing their views, no matter how controversial they may be.
- Make sure managers across the organization do the same.
- Take visible action on other people's ideas.

Follow Communication Best Practices

- Adopt a crisis management mindset, especially if the strategy represents a material change compared to the past:
  - Be frequent—it's okay to communicate on a weekly basis.
  - Be concise—focus on facts and metrics and be specific.
  - Be relevant—focus on what matters for your employees.
  - Be consistent—announce your cadence of communication and stick to it.
  - Be honest—don't make false promises; explain what is known and unknown.
  - Be confident—people look up to you for leadership; speak accordingly.

▶ Be compassionate—acknowledge that employees may be struggling.

Manage Change

- Recognize that leaders (yourself and your leadership team) are several steps ahead of employees when it comes to embracing change.
- Address the emotional and behavioral aspects along operational dimensions.
- Change unfolds in a reasonably predictable and manageable series of phases; identify which stage you're in and act accordingly.
- Become familiar with a reliable change framework (e.g. *The Change Monster* by Jeanie Duck).

CHAPTER 7

The Third Key:
Balanced Metrics

Metrics That Matter

Metrics are important for alignment and execution. They help you focus and avoid distraction once the strategy and market discipline have been set, and they help measure progress and motivate employees. But just because we *can* measure something in a business doesn't mean we *should*. As William Bruce Cameron said in a quote often attributed to Albert Einstein, "Not everything that counts can be counted, and not everything that can be counted counts."

How does a business leader determine what *does* need to be measured? What metrics will provide meaningful information? The purpose of your company's balanced metrics is to help you reach your desired outcomes.

A great lesson in this for me occurred at a West Coast mortgage company we had been working with. The company had grown through acquisitions over the previous five years and was struggling to realize the expected synergies, while facing a substantial drop in the volume of mortgages.

To identify the issues facing the company, we applied the model behind our Line-of-Sight methodology. After sending out the assessment to all the employees and analyzing the results with the leadership team, we traced back the main challenge to a significant and rather simple misalignment in their performance metrics. In particular, their pipeline reporting was tracking application volumes prior to qualification; however, a substantial number of applicants were rejected after the customary screening in some of their regions. An updated reporting was put in place, tracking the pipeline pre- and post-qualification. This allowed the company to benchmark acceptance rates across its units to establish more effective and consistent qualification tests, refine its sales and marketing model to target more promising applicants, and run the integrated organization with more reliable data.

Better reporting also addressed another consequence of poorly defined metrics: a serious gap in accountability. Unsurprisingly, unreliable metrics had meant that it was difficult to hold anyone responsible for performance. The improvement in metrics also helped clarify who was in charge of meeting performance goals.

You should obviously focus on metrics that track the value drivers unique to your industry and do so in a way that protects and supports your business model. Here is a telling story about the unintended consequences of poorly chosen metrics: One of my fellow Line-of-Sight owners previously led a high-end grocery store chain. Their operating motto was "Food for fun, not food for fuel," and their focus was on delivering an amazing customer experience. Customer intimacy was the foundation of their approach, which meant that all associates, including the CEO, were expected to spend a lot of time in the stores, observing, engaging, and helping customers—up to 50 percent of their time for store managers. In fact, they did not call customers "customers"; they called them "guests."

The company was very analytical, tracking items as detailed and precise as the return per square inch of their weekly ads. In a bid to further boost performance and get an ever more detailed view of its operations, the chain decided to roll out a new, comprehensive dashboard with 93 different Key Performance Indicators. Within the first month of its introduction, the dashboard's complexity led store managers to forgo their time on the floor to focus on understanding and analyzing every metric and be ready to explain them in new monthly management and review meetings. Within three months, customer satisfaction survey results had plummeted, as store managers and their associates were shifting their attention away from customers and toward internal operations. It was also apparent that many of the indicators did not provide any guidance on how to run stores efficiently. Take the example of these two metrics included in the dashboard:

- Sales per square foot of the department: this metric was helpful for future store design and layout; however, it was not useful nor actionable for daily store level execution.
- Items per minute (IPM): this indicator measured the speed of the cashier. But be careful what you ask for: after a few weeks, it turned out that cashiers were indeed paying attention to the metric; unfortunately, it also became clear that the higher the IPM, the lower the guest engagement scores.

By month four, the new dashboard had been trimmed down to eleven KPIs, reversing the erosion of the in-store customer experience and giving everyone their sanity back. This was another case of "less is more"; the 11 KPIs focused on the underlying drivers of performance in support of delighting customers, and ditched everything else. Here are some of these eleven metrics:

- Guests waiting in line (GWIL): a critical data point for delivering on a "high touch" guest service strategy.
- Items per order (IPO): a measure of the store's merchandising prowess (one or two more items in each basket has a huge return)
- Carts in the parking lot (CPL): first impressions are made walking into the store; 15 cart maximum in the lot at any given time
- Out of Stocks (OOS): You can't sell what you don't have. Focus on minimizing and rapid recovery led to industry-leading performance in stock position to maximize sales.

Metrics Begin with the End in Sight

When you start with the end in sight, you're more likely to get to your destination!

Sometimes, an area of misalignment can be a significant disconnect between the budget and the strategy. When that's the case, financial and human capital aren't allocated where they're most needed. Here again, strategy dictates the priorities for both financial capital and human capital.

Sometimes, internal jockeying among executives or competing departmental requests might move the budget off-kilter by sprinkling resources across too many areas —another expression of a lack of focus. The only priority that matters is whatever will move the needle in a favorable direction. What will best accomplish the organization's mission? Spending decisions should be driven by what creates an advantage in the marketplace through the right market discipline: your metrics must align with your business model—operational excellence, innovation, or customer intimacy.

In chapter 1, we discussed the founder's trap, the growth challenge that might arise when the entrepreneurial leader who built the company still runs it the way they've always been comfortable doing, despite a larger organization and changing circumstances. I have noticed they might often continue to run the company by instinct. They don't necessarily utilize or analyze metrics against objectives, and rarely use dashboards showing aggregate performance data across their value chain.

It is no wonder than when business owners sell to a larger entity or a private equity firm, one of the first actions of the buyer is often to enforce greater accountability by rolling out a new dashboard backed by clear goals. Private equity firms like to say "we buy chaos at an discount and sell order at a premium"—and order starts with metrics that provide effective control.

Good Metrics

The rule of thumb is to ask yourself what you intend to learn by measuring. If you learn what you intended to, will you do anything differently? If the answer is yes, measure away. But if the answer is no, it's not worth measuring. With metrics more than anything, less is more (Fig. 7.1).

A good place to start is to think in terms of lagging and leading indicators.

Lagging indicators provide insights into past events and outcomes. They are useful to evaluate the effectiveness of your strategy or how well you are performing against goals. They will also help you identify trends by providing historical data, and benchmark your performance against your industry or peers, using their own historical data.

Balanced Metrics

General Prescriptions

- Ensure you are measuring the right things
- Track both leading and lagging indicators
- Develop KPIs that drive desirable behavior
- Stop measuring the stuff that doesn't move the needle

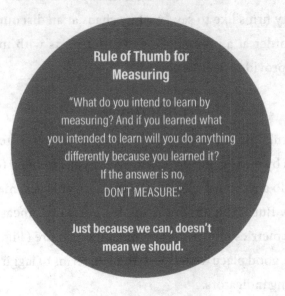

Rule of Thumb for Measuring

"What do you intend to learn by measuring? And if you learned what you intended to learn will you do anything differently because you learned it?
If the answer is no,
DON'T MEASURE."

Just because we can, doesn't mean we should.

Fig. 7.1. Prescriptions to develop balanced metrics

They are a good indicator of the overall health of the organization. The typical performance metrics used to discuss a company's performance are lagging metrics, such as:

- Revenues
- Margins

- Market share
- Customer satisfaction
- Quality
- Safety
- Employee engagement

Leading indicators provide insights into future outcomes. They are particularly critical when you operate in an uncertain environment where past performance is not a reliable indicator for the future.

Leading indicators are predictive; they are designed to provide early information or signals about the future performance of aspects of the organization, so that decisions can be made in time to influence results. Leading indicators are typically more granular than lagging indicators; they will focus on specific drivers that are known to impact performance. For example, the monthly sales pipeline is a leading indicator for sales, but not the only factor that will determine the eventual revenues for the period; however, it is one of the elements that influence the overall sales and is actionable. If the pipeline points to weakening sales, the organization can run a promotion, a new marketing campaign, or engage some recurring clients with special renewal offers.

Leading indicators include metrics such as:

- Number of qualified leads in the sales pipeline
- Sales activity, e.g. number of outbound calls, or meetings scheduled by salespeople
- Inventory turnover
- Supplier risk (which determined revenues when disrupted supply chains during the pandemic caused finished products to be held for lack of specific parts)

Leading indicators require careful analysis; you need to understand whether and how they actually impact the outcomes you want to influence. For example, if you are trying to improve safety in your operations, you need to understand its drivers: Is it employee compliance with the use of personal protective equipment? Is it the number of hours of safety training programs?

Typically, leading metrics will be unique to particular industries. For example, I helped a client improve the safety record of their delivery truck drivers: we analyzed the behavioral profile of drivers and identified that drivers that were more risk-averse and exhibited higher patience (i.e. worked at a steady pace) and formality (tended to respect rules and structure) had less accidents. Therefore, historical analysis using a lagging indicator (safety record) helped identify a leading indicator (driver profile) that became a predictor for future safety performance. The client could proactively make hiring decisions using that insight, which improved their safety record, resulting in lower claim costs and higher customer satisfaction.

You can see that the same metrics can simultaneously be leading and lagging indicators. For example, employee satisfaction is a lagging indicator: it results from factors such as the quality of the managers, the good fit between employees and their jobs, how much employees trust their leadership, or the clarity of the company's purpose, as we discussed earlier. At the same time, it is also a predictor of employee turnover and productivity—even if other drivers also influence these outcomes.

Missing Metrics

Beware: the *absence* of metrics and data for the things that matter most also presents problems. Though it's difficult to notice an absence, that's the point! Be on the lookout for areas that your measurements and information system overlook partly or entirely. For example, let's consider a manufacturing company looking to develop an new application. It sounds logical that it should capture data about the potential customer segments, their needs, buying habits, etc. However, in our experience, many companies surprisingly struggle to gather data and metrics on their actual or prospective customers. More often than not, they rely on their own assumptions ("we know our customers better than they know themselves!") or stereotypes and rarely look externally. IDEO, the design firm, built the design-thinking methodology to truly walk in the shoes of customers beyond biases and assumptions—and this is surprisingly hard to achieve. If you don't know what you don't know about your customers, and don't have metrics and insights to keep yourself honest, you are likely to miss the mark.

Factors that are challenging to measure are nevertheless important to your company's success. For example, it isn't easy to quantify employee engagement. If you do not ask the right questions that focus on the areas where employees may be struggling, you will miss warning signs; you will also have biased insights if you cannot guarantee 100 percent anonymity. This is why it makes sense to use specialized engagement measurement tools rather than trying to create your own on Google Forms or SurveyMonkey, as so many companies do.

Too Much Information or Too Little Analysis

Just because something is quantifiable doesn't mean it should be measured. Metrics must be meaningful to shape your organization's behavior, and having too many confuses employees as to which metric they should optimize. Focus on what matters most!

When we operate in an uncertain environment, we can be tempted to try and gather more data to help with decisions. However, a healthy organization is like a smooth-running car that measures what the driver needs to know—speed, gas level, distance, and so on. Extraneous measurements can distract the driver. Does your dashboard need to show you the rate at which the car's paint is fading in the sun, or the number of vehicles it passes on the highway? If presented with too much information, people will ignore it or become confused, even at the leadership level, at which point you run the risk of losing them. You must also weigh the value of data against the time and resources necessary to collect and analyze it. Collecting information is only the first step. A spreadsheet or list of numbers may look impressive, but it's useless if no one knows how to analyze it. The process requires expertise to maximize its efficacy.

The most important questions are: (1) Are your metrics meaningful and balanced between leading and lagging indicators? (2) Are you conducting thoughtful analysis of the numbers? (3) Will the data yield information that simplifies the executives' job and meets their expectations? (4) Can we you derive actions when metrics don't meet standards and goals?

If the answers are yes, buckle up your seatbelt and enjoy the ride to execution excellence.

Visible Metrics

Regardless of the metrics you select, they should be visible to employees.

You can display them in real time on monitors around the office, or share them in weekly, monthly, or quarterly meetings, or via email. Access to the key measures is what creates an environment of self-inspection and self-correction: when employees can measure their performance, they can take action to improve it.

> Self–inspection leads
> to self–correction.

Think of your employees as athletes: it would be inconceivable that an athlete running around the track would not have access to their running time. Give your employees access to the data they need in order to know

where they stand, and help them take action to improve
their performance and therefore that of the company.

In this chapter we discussed:

1. Metrics are important for business alignment, execution, measuring progress, and motivating employees.
2. Ask yourself what you intend to learn by measuring and whether it will drive any different behavior and be actionable.
3. Balanced metrics are crucial, incorporating both leading and lagging indicators.
4. Less is more: just because you can measure something does not mean you should.
5. Be mindful of your blind spots, i.e. areas of your value chain where you don't know what you don't know.
6. Weigh the value of insights against the time and resources necessary to collect and analyze them.

(ONE MORE THING)

An Additional Perspective on Metrics

We always enjoy it when a world-class consultancy like McKinsey affirms our perspective on execution. This was the case in a podcast episode in which McKinsey experts discussed all things execution with Workboard co-founder and CEO Deidre Paknad.[14]

In this chapter, we've emphasized that one of the keys to successful execution is to have clear metrics. We often think of metrics as a way to understand the health of the business, but an even more critical role for metrics is to guide employees' behavior into doing the things that matter. Metrics should remove any ambiguity as to what needs to be done.

In the podcast, Paknad made the case for using simple Objective and Key Results (OKRs) metrics to do exactly that. Let's review how OKRs work and why they are so useful compared to traditional business metrics.

What does it take to execute well?

Strategy execution is simple: you need clear market discipline (understanding how you compete in your market), a well-defined strategy, and complete

ONE MORE THING

alignment of your people and resources with your goals.

You gain execution alignment when a relatively small number of conditions are met:

- All employees (not just the leadership team) understand the strategy.
- The leadership is trusted to manage execution.
- Daily activities are directly relevant to the strategy, and the company structure makes it easy to perform them.
- Talent is recruited and developed to directly support the strategy.
- And finally, metrics guide employees in their daily decisions to focus on what is important.

In other words, these are the five Keys to Strategic Execution, or KSE, with which you are now familiar.

Out of the five KSEs, metrics are notoriously challenging: there are often too many of them, they may not be explicit enough to inform decisions and behaviors, and their collection and analysis may take valuable time and resources away from execution.

This is why Paknad's advice to focus only on a small number of OKRs is so refreshing and effective

┌─────────[**ONE MORE THING**]─────────┐

for execution. It also yields many benefits compared to traditional metrics.

What are OKRs?

OKRs are outcomes that a team or an entire organization wants to achieve, typically within the next ninety days.

OKRs differ from regular business goals in several ways:

- There should be a very small number of OKRs. Paknad suggests no more than three to five objectives and four to five key results for each objective.
- The ninety-day short-term horizon forces teams to focus on what will make the biggest impact on their performance.
- They are re-evaluated every ninety days, which makes them well suited for environments where change happens fast.

Think of OKR as the "metric of the realist": it acknowledges that most organizations are constrained in terms of time, money, resources, and people; it forces everyone top to bottom to focus on what will yield the biggest result within these constraints.

As Paknad says, "The objectives are a statement of intention. What is it we're trying to accomplish? Do the key results cover what is success in the next ninety days? What will we have more of or less of?"[15]

Less is more.

As Paknad puts it, "The inability to know what matters most right now is a huge drain for organizations."[16]

Leaders are often told that their organization should operate like a start-up to be nimble and grow fast, and "keep their eyes on the ball." In reality this is very hard to achieve, as organizational complexity increases with scale, and many balls end up competing for everyone's attention.

OKR may be the best way to replicate the environment in which entrepreneurs operate and fight complexity; this is an easy-to-use device to be laser-focused on what will generate the biggest results in the shortest amount of time and within the scarce resources at hand.

Your Organization's Health Index Evaluation: Balanced Metrics

Use this rating scale to assess the execution capabilities of your organization in the table below:

A: Aligned (5 points)   M: Misaligned (-1 point)
S: Somewhat Aligned (2 points)   N: Not Sure (0 points)

Index	Balanced Metrics Health Assessment Criteria	Your Assessment (A, S, M, N)	Your Score (5, 2, -1, 0 point)
BM1	My organization uses a balanced set of leading and lagging indicators and measurements.		
BM2	My immediate team's key performance indicators help team members stay focused on delivering unique customer value.		
BM3	We link budgets to our organization's overall strategy. (Budgets help us make decisions that support our strategy.)		
BM4	My immediate team is aware of and has access to measurements and metrics that help us perform our jobs better.		

Total Score _____

From a Balanced Metrics standpoint, the health of your organization is as follows:

- If your total score is 10 or less, your organization is not feeling well.

- If your score is between 10 and 17, your organization is going about its day but is not able to run a sprint without feeling depleted.
- If your score is 17 or above, your organization is very fit. It can tackle any challenge that the world throws at it.

Balanced Metrics Prescriptions
If Your Health Score Is 15 or Below
Use Leading and Lagging Indicators

- As the name suggests, balanced metrics should incorporate a mix of leading and lagging indicators:
  - ▸ Leading indicators are predictive measures that help forecast where the company will go. Typically, a leading indicator is a piece of economic data that correlates with change in a variable of interest to the company. For example, changes in consumer confidence may correlate with demand for the services that the company offers; employee satisfaction may be a leading indicator of customer satisfaction. Leading indicators help forecast revenues and other elements of performance.
  - ▸ Lagging indicators help measure progress by looking at past performance. For example, customer satisfaction indicates how well the company performs.

- ▸ A balance of leading and lagging indicators is necessary: leading indicators help determine the potential of the company, and lagging indicators help assess how that potential has been achieved.
- Use the analogy of the car: when driving a car, the person at the wheel looks both backward through the rearview mirror and forward through the windshield. What they see will influence how they drive and where they're going. Similarly, when driving the future of a company, the leader must look backward to measure past and current performance and ahead to determine how to produce desired results.

Use a Small Number of Metrics

- Less is more: tie metrics only to strategic goals:
  - ▸ If you are using OKRs (Objectives and Key Results), make sure that you can track the four to five key results for each objective.
- Remove "legacy" metrics that have been tracked for a long time but are not actively used.
- Avoid sedimentation: remove a metric for any new metric you add.

Test New Metrics

- Stress-test each metric to make sure it is actionable:

- ▸ Does the metric accurately track the underlying variable it is supposed to?
- ▸ Is the measurement process reliable?
- ▸ Does it require human data input or intervention?
- ▸ Is the reporting happening on a timely basis?
- ▸ Does the intended audience understand the metric, what it tracks, and what should be done based on the posted values?

Anticipate the Impact of Metrics

- Anticipate the behaviors that each metric will foster among employees:
  - ▸ Will these behaviors contribute to our strategic goals?
  - ▸ Is there a risk of unanticipated consequences?

Make Sure Metrics Are Visible

- To be acted upon by employees, metrics must be visible. Make sure metrics reach their intended audience (either the entire organization or specific teams).
  - ▸ Make sure dashboards are accessible to their audience; either pushed or pulled on demand.
  - ▸ Consider posting dashboards visibly across the organization and/or in each area where specific metrics are relevant: screens in public spaces, meeting rooms, etc.

Be a Role Model for the Use of Metrics

- Use metrics in your regular communication to employees.
- Review dashboards on a timely basis.
- Ask questions about metrics to employees; show that you pay attention, and confirm that they understand what the metrics mean.

The Fourth Key: Activities (of Employees) and Structure (of Your Organization)

Strategy Before Structure

Focusing on the people who do the lion's share of the day-to-day work to execute your strategy goes hand-in-hand with focusing on organizational structure. Structure takes various forms, including the flow of communication, procedures, systems, use of technology, and the accountability and reporting chart.

> Many leaders might mistakenly think that the organizational structure is independent from their strategy.

A company needs to know its vision *before* determining what organizational structure will help execute it. *What* you intend to do determines *who* will be the best people to do it—and how they should be organized (see Fig. 8.1).

Therefore, the organizational structure should be determined by the strategy. A few years ago, I worked with the leadership team of a law firm who wanted to redesign their organizational structure; the husband and wife founders, after many years of hard work to build their firm to a healthy size, wanted to take a step back from the business and start focusing on their work-life balance. Their initial succession plan was to progressively transfer their responsibilities to their two daughters. But behind this succession plan was the implicit recognition that the firm's future success would depend on its ability to navigate a very different operating business environment going forward, with more complex legal matters, more intense competition, and greater use of technology and outsourced resources.

Activities & Structure

General Prescriptions

- **Keep It Simple:** Adopt a structure consistent with your market discipline
- **Growth Plan:** Is the right reporting structure in place to grow?
- **Relevance:** Are you performing the few key things flawlessly that set you apart?
- **Exclusive Focus:** "The essence of strategy lies in choosing what not to do." (Michael Porter)

Fig. 8.1. Prescriptions for activities and structure

It became clear that the growth strategy of the firm needed to be clarified before any organizational decision could be made. So we conducted several strategy sessions to set the vision, goals, and strategy first. When that was done, we then moved to define the optimal organization that could execute that strategy; we decided that splitting responsibilities between the family daughters was the best approach, with one running operational aspects and the other focused on growing the book of business and managing client relationships. However, we also determined that the firm needed more robust leadership at all levels and a solid development plan to cultivate the future managers and experts of the firm. So the firm also put in place an internal employee development program, added a new mid-management layer to create more development opportunities for future leaders, and started to thoughtfully shape the culture to be more participative—all of which set the firm on a solid path for sustained growth.

Does this example sound familiar? This is an example of the founder's trap. If you do not focus on goals first, it will be difficult to organize your operations without paying a big execution tax, in the form of redundant accountabilities, lack of collaboration, or poorly designed processes. Strategy must come before structure.

Which Structure to Implement?

Company size is obviously a criteria to determine the right organizational model. In general, it is best to have as little complexity as possible by keeping reporting and communication lines short, with as few hierarchy layers as possible. This facilitates and accelerates decision-making and keeps everyone informed on a timely basis. This "flat" structure is well-suited for smaller organizations. It is also an effective model for organizations that depend on speed for success, whether they are in the early stages of growth, operate in a high-velocity industry, or face a crisis that demands high-stake decisions to be made under pressure with as much collective insights as possible. Regardless of the context, in this model individual and team activities are determined by the collective knowledge of the group, with good visibility and understanding of what other people are doing: individuals can easily define their respective roles and responsibilities without overlap.

Especially when market discipline is about innovation, there are advantages to having a decentralized structure where functional units have significant freedom of action. Their activities are determined by their own deep understanding of what needs to be done in their own area of responsibility, and by their close proximity with the market or technology development. Then again, it is

also possible to achieve innovation with a more centralized model: as we saw earlier, Apple has a centralized
decision-making model that ensures the integrity of its
product innovation strategy and guarantees that all parts
of the organization work in tight coordination to deliver
the vision behind its product development. In this model,
individual activities are informed by the overall vision of
the organization acting as the framework for innovation,
either as a catalyst (making sure the product vision is
pushed despite challenges) or constraint (narrowing the
focus to only the product plan and technology develop-
ments determined at the enterprise level).

If your market discipline is built around operational
excellence, consider organizing your structure function-
ally to maximize domain expertise and the continuous
optimization of systems and processes for efficiency. In
this model, activities are driven by efficiency metrics
providing deep insights and a clear path of action for each
functional area.

Conversely, if your market discipline is built around
customer intimacy, what matters is to capture and dissem-
inate customer knowledge and intimacy deep inside the
organization. A cross-functional organization where
teams bring together different functions and perspectives
is a good solution to spur that dissemination and foster

collaboration. Teams can be organized along processes or dimensions of the customer experience (for example, "How do we deliver a seamless payment experience to each client?"). In this case, individual activities are naturally focused on the satisfaction of client needs, and informed by the broad understanding of the factors that influence it. That model is effective when the performance of your organization is dependent on having a system view of things—understanding and managing multiple and interdependent drivers. This is also a good model for temporary project teams that need to bring different skills together.

The personal goals of the founder/leader and their succession plans may also influence the organizational model. For example, one of our clients, a thirty-five-person manufacturing company, has a flat organization with a small six-person leadership team as the main layer between the CEO and employees. The owner has been deeply involved in the most critical aspects of the operations, which are supply chain and procurement and manufacturing; yet, as he considered his future plans to sell the business or scale down his day-to-day involvement, he strategically hired new talent in those areas to build a deeper bench in these functions and free up his own attention to refocus on other projects that do not have a specific functional owner, like the rollout of a new ERP system. In addition, he has provided professional coaching support to his leadership team; with that support, the team is transforming from a functional team, where each member is primarily focused on reporting on their own area (working "in the business"), to a strategic team able to work collaboratively "on the business" and make the type of decisions that until then only the owner would make. This hybrid model is therefore part functional and part cross-functional; team members balance their activities between their functional responsibilities (optimizing the performance of their department) and their collective responsibility as stewards of the overall company—or at least as an effective though and accountability partner of the CEO.

Naturally, the reporting structure needs to match the organizational structure. Regardless of how they are set up, the organizational units (e.g. teams, units, divisions) must have access to metrics, data, and performance reports that measure their performance and allow them to make decisions accordingly: as I often say, *self-inspection drives self-correction*.

As we've discussed throughout this book, business success depends on complete alignment across all strata of the organization. Implementing these recommendations does not require a big investment; instead, it involves time, understanding, communication, and follow-through. The results will be quickly evident in the effective execution of your strategy.

In the next chapter, we'll continue the conversation about your most valuable asset: your people. We'll see how employee engagement relates to recruitment and retention.

In this chapter we discussed:

1. A company needs to know its vision before determining which organizational structure will help execute it.
2. The structure should be determined based on the company size, the market discipline it is competing with (innovation, operational excellence, or customer intimacy), and the long-term succession plans for the business owner.
3. If you compete based on innovation, consider a decentralized structure that offers freedom of action to functional units.
4. If your market discipline is built around operational excellence, consider a functional structure in which functions can focus on building their domain expertise and continuously optimize systems and processes.
5. If your market discipline is built around customer intimacy, consider a cross-functional organization that shares insights into the customer behavior and quickly adapts to evolving needs.

ONE MORE THING

An Additional Perspective on Activities and Structure

If your company underwent drastic changes in its strategy or operating model since the pandemic years, you are not alone. Back in 2020, garment companies started to produce face masks, and appliance manufacturers churned out respirators. Not every CEO made such dramatic shifts in their operations, but many of us needed to reorient our goals and execution to survive and thrive.

In addition, some sectors have experienced fundamental shifts accelerated by the pandemic that will most likely be permanent. For example, mall operators have seen a radical shift in consumer behavior relative to in-person shopping; car manufacturers are facing a permanent transition to electric mobility.

The question is: If your strategy changed, should your organization change too? Do you need to execute differently? The answer is yes.

(ONE MORE THING)

Different Goals, Different Execution:
the Harley–Davidson LiveWire Story

Harley-Davidson is one of the most iconic brands in the world. Like many global brands, its appeal is grounded in consumer perceptions about tradition and the permanence of its values.

Tradition can be an asset, but when it comes to the transition the motorcycle market is under-going, Harley-Davidson was at risk of staying mired in producing increasingly outdated products in the middle of a fundamental shift to electric mobility.

Harley-Davidson saw the opportunity and launched an electric motorcycle, the LiveWire, which existed alongside their line-up for some time. But Harley-Davidson realized it could not properly execute its electric strategy while still focusing on its more traditional bikes. As a result, it announced in December 2021 that it would spin off LiveWire as an entire brand and operations.

One Goal, Well Executed

Harley-Davidson's story is not isolated. Ford Motor Company made a similar announcement for the same reason: the execution capabilities to support

---

(ONE MORE THING)

a strategy based on innovation (in HD's case, transitioning to electric bikes) cannot durably co-exist with those required to enable a strategy based on efficiencies at scale. While Harley-Davidson has has not revealed much about LiveWire's set up, we can expect that many execution aspects are different from their traditional, scale-based operations:

- Strategic goals and metrics geared toward innovation and speed-to-market vs. production volume
- Leadership more focused on empowering teams for creativity
- Flatter structure, more cross-functional to accelerate problem resolution in the face of new challenges
- Talent: more electrical engineers, battery experts, materials specialists

Harley-Davidson rightly understood that execution and strategy must be in sync. In fact, they did not choose one strategy over the other: they intended to maximize the remaining potential of the traditional large bike market while building market leadership in electric bikes, but they identified the risk of pursuing

ONE MORE THING

two very different strategies with a single execution model.

What Are You Trying To Do and How Well Are You Doing It?

Not every company needs to spin off part of its operations to succeed, but every company CEO should be crystal clear about their goals and able to determine whether they are executing them well.

One Line-of-Sight client is a large family office- and wealth-management firm. Employees' morale was low, and the firm struggled to reach its goals for assets under management. After running a health scan on their operations, they realized they were, in fact, pursuing two very different segments with a single operating model: on one end, high net-worth individuals requiring individual touch and a delivery model based on customer intimacy, and on the other end, mid-market clients who needed to be serviced at scale to be profitable. The mix of high-service and phone-based support was inadequate for either segment, costing both sales and profit.

After a comprehensive review of their execution capabilities, they set up two delivery models in two

╭─────────────[**ONE MORE THING**]─────────────╮

divisions for their two segments: a customer intimacy-based model to serve clients with very high investable income and an operational excellence-based model for mid-market. As a result, the firm increased their retention in both segments, and they doubled their assets under management despite the pandemic.

Where to Start

If you feel that your operating model and your strategy are increasingly at odds, run a health scan to evaluate how clearly you have articulated your strategy (to yourself, to your executive team, and to your employees), and how much your structure is enabling or preventing success. Are employees focusing on the right things, and are you helping them do so? It's okay to develop new goals when circumstances demand it, but goals and execution should remain in lockstep.

╰───╯

Your Organization's Health Index Evaluation:
Activities and Structure

Use this rating scale to assess the execution capabilities of your organization in the table below:

A: Aligned (5 points)   **M: Misaligned (-1 point)**
S: Somewhat Aligned (2 points) **N: Not Sure (0 points)**

Index	Activities and Structure Health Assessment Criteria	Your Assessment (A, S, M, N)	Your Score (5, 2, -1, 0 point)
AS1	Leaders use our company's strategy as a tool for helping employees stay focused on the critical few tasks that bring the most value to the company.		
AS2	We use our knowledge of the strategy to help prioritize our daily activity and task list.		
AS3	Our company's organization chart and structure support the strategy.		
AS4	My immediate team understands how our efforts, decisions, and actions lead to creating unique customer value.		

Total Score _____

From an Activities and Structure standpoint, the health of your organization is as follows:

- If your total score is 10 or less, your organization is not feeling well.

- If your score is between 10 and 17, your organization is going about its day but is not able to run a sprint without feeling depleted.
- If your score is 17 or above, your organization is very fit. It can tackle any challenge that the world throws at it.

Activities and Structure Prescriptions If Your Health Score Is 17 or Below

Align the Structure with Market Discipline

- The structure of the organization should reflect the market discipline that the company pursues. For example, the strategy will determine the structure's characteristics as follows:

  ▶ Operational Excellence strategy: Institute cross-functional teams that are able to consider each process's performance end-to-end and are able to eliminate process breakdowns that may occur along functional lines.

  ▶ Product Innovation strategy: Institute a flat organization designed to accelerate decision-making.

  ▶ Customer Intimacy strategy: Institute a rotational program designed to expose leaders and executives to various customer-facing functions.

Determine Key Activities

- Consider the end-to-end processes required to deliver the activities (rather than functional lines).
- Eliminate activities and tasks that do not contribute to strategic outcomes.
- Then, assess which part of the organization should be accountable for each of the activities and processes.

Evaluate and Design the Organization with Outcomes in Mind

For each of the outcomes sought by the strategy, what is the most effective way:

- To share strategic objectives, tactical guidance, and data with employees about which tasks to focus on?
- To have employees share feedback and ideas about their tasks?
- To shield employees from interference that may disrupt their focus on key activities?
- To share leading and lagging indicators with employees for them to optimize their own performance?
- To ensure that employees understand how their actions and efforts create unique customer value?

The Fifth Key: People (Human Capital)

Your employees are a precious resource that should be treated like platinum—we already discussed how you should follow the platinum rule when engaging others: treat others like they want to be treated, not like you'd want to be treated. This attitude goes a long way to retaining your company's talent.

Here's a great example. A home healthcare company was experiencing higher-than-expected turnover in the patient care technician role. More than 80 percent of the employees in the company were patient care technicians, and this rise in turnover was having a significant impact on their ability to service existing customers. It was crippling their ability to grow. Using the insights from their health scan, they took a two-step approach to the problem.

First, they completely overhauled their talent acquisition process, added behavioral analytics into the hiring process, clearly defined the role, and added structured interviewing to ensure they were hiring the right people for the role.

Second, a ninety-day onboarding process was implemented, with daily touches for the first two weeks and weekly meetings for the next three months. Learnings from these onboarding meetings led to a change in scheduling, from one-week schedules to two-week schedules.

These changes led to significant improvement in turnover, with retention rates at an all-time high. We'll discuss the question of employee retention later in this chapter. But first, we'll look at the measurable task of attracting the best talent for your organization.

The Right Person, in the Right Role, at the Right Time, Doing the Right Thing Right

Human capital refers to "the skills, knowledge, and health that people invest in and accumulate throughout their lives."[17] When employers recruit talent, they need to look for people who possess the attributes most compatible with the roles they seek to fill. They need people who have the right "human capital" to execute the company's unique customer value proposition and strategy.

Psychometrics evaluate an individual's cognitive and behavioral characteristics. Many psychometric assessment tools are available to specifically determine the work-related personality attributes that predict whether an employee or job candidate is the right person for the role. The results are valuable for employers making hiring decisions because they bring objectivity to behaviors, such as the pace at which someone works, their appetite for risk, how they best communicate, what environment they thrive in, how they approach decision-making, and how they solve problems.

We use a tool called the Predictive Index Behavioral Assessment, which has been used for decades and has been the subject of nearly five hundred validation studies. As the company itself states, the Predictive Index Behavioral Assessment (BA) is a well-established, business-relevant, and scientifically proven measure of behavioral tendencies in the workplace.

The Predictive Index founder, Arnold Daniels, was an airman with the US Air Force in World War II. Sent to England as a navigator in bombing missions over occupied Europe, he and his crew logged an unprecedented number of missions without casualties, attracting the attention of the US Air Force, which sent a psychologist to understand the crew's performance and document best practices. This was the start of Daniels's lifelong mission to understand individual behavior and its impact on performance. He released the first version of his psychometrics assessment in 1952 and founded the Predictive Index in 1955. Since then, more than forty million people have taken the Predictive Index Behavioral Assessment. The BA is an easy-to-administer six-minute assessment, and the results make the otherwise subjective hiring and development process an objective, data-based, effective one. It measures "four drives that determine workplace behavior": dominance (drive to influence people and events), extraversion (drive for social interaction), patience (drive for consistency and stability), and formality (drive to conform to rules and structure).[18] The assessment consists of only two questions with free choice responses that ask you to pick among adjectives to describe how others perceive you and how you perceive yourself.

We've found that using the BA reliably helps companies find job candidates with the suitable drives to perform a particular role. Administering the BA at the outset of the hiring and development process saves companies valuable time on interviewing and reduces the risk of a mis-hire. And if the candidate is otherwise desirable but has gaps that may negatively affect performance, the employer (typically the supervisor) has the data required to provide the right development and coaching.

Our team of Line-of-Sight consultants typically integrate the BA into our execution alignment program. We conduct BA evaluations along with the Line-of-Sight assessment that offers insight into how a company is executing its strategy. These assessments give us a complete picture of your company's needs. The Predictive Index can be used for the entire lifecycle of an employee—hopefully, a long, healthy one—from job creation, attracting candidates, performance management, to conflict resolution and career development.

Your Passport to Retention: Learning and Development

Once you've hired the right candidate, you want to keep them! You need to set a new employee up for success the moment that they begin work. This means leading your right employee the right way. Critical considerations include how you onboard them, how you initially train them, and how you continually develop their talent.

Once again, let's remember the platinum rule: treat your employees the way they want to be treated. This rule applies to training and coaching your employees the way that is most effective *for them*.

Consider the unique behavioral needs of operators on the floor of a manufacturing company. While you'll find many different employee profiles depending on the technology used—the production model, etc.—in my experience these employees are generally patient, focused, detail- and process-oriented. They favor stability and familiarity with procedures to execute tasks in the right way—deviating from the standard might have bad consequences for operator safety. These employees are rarely risk-takers or big innovators—it just does not work for these roles. To effectively train and coach these employees, it's important to develop a sustained, well-organized program that is predictable, with the agenda communicated well in advance. Ideally, trainers and coaches will remain the same throughout the program; concepts will be covered several times and in depth.

In contrast, salespeople might be more excited about new ideas and may not require as much advance notice or detailed information. Markets change, customer needs change, products change, and the company must adapt. Again, you treat different populations differently because their behavioral wiring isn't the same. Learning and development (L&D) initiatives must also be tailored to the person and the position's requirements.

Managers and leaders require a high degree of self-awareness and awareness of others, whether they interact with frontline factory operators or executives.

Starting off on the Right Foot with Onboarding

Onboarding is critical for many reasons: it sets the tone for the rest of the employee's tenure, it contributes to making a good first impression, and it eases and accelerates the ramp-up of the employee on their way to be a full-fledged, productive, engaged member of the company workforce. Here are a few simple, good practices to keep in mind:

- Have the employee's manager reach out before they start; many studies show that manager outreach has an outsized importance on the new employee perception of the support they will receive when they join; similarly, make sure the manager meets or talks to the new employee on their first day on the job.
- Give the manager the behavioral pattern and analysis of the new employee; it will help them welcome them and lead them accordingly, from day one.

- As we saw before, culture is key: make sure to discuss the mission, vision, and strategic intent of the company in the first few days, and ideally on day one.
- If possible, personalize the onboarding process to the behavioral needs of the new employee: some people like to get information in advance (send them a welcome package with all the details); some people learn through social interaction (make sure they meet many of their colleagues during onboarding).

Passport, Please

One method we've pioneered to train employees and provide continuing education for them is a "passport program." Once you've defined the core competencies necessary for a role, you must tailor the training accordingly. Each role is unique. We've designed a tri-fold handout (called "passport") that lists various milestones for week one, thirty days, sixty days, and up to 180 days to ensure an employee achieves the necessary competencies in a timely manner. The passport pace and structure are tailored to the employee's profile. Another benefit of this program is that employees are held accountable throughout the process.

As we just saw, the starting point for everyone—from frontline factory operators to vice president of sales—is learning the company's mission, vision, and strategy. The next steps for a factory employee may be working side by side with an experienced worker. For new salespeople, it may be shadowing a peer, gaining product knowledge, visiting a factory floor, and so on. We are big believers in the apprenticeship model.

Supporting and continually educating your employees so they succeed goes a long way toward retention. Remember: employees are more likely to be engaged if they feel good about themselves, about their jobs, about their managers, and they find purpose in their work.

Hiring the wrong candidate or having the right people leave your company are both costly. Peter Scholtes, a former priest turned management consultant, formulated two questions employers need to ask themselves about non-performing employees: "Why did we hire dead wood? Or why did we hire live wood and kill it?"[19] To hire the right people, retain them and then train and treat them the right way. To ensure they stay engaged contributors to your company, use a behavioral assessment like BA.

The Generation Gap

People react to current events differently depending on their age, education, and so on. Therefore, employers should be responsive to the general trends and needs of

each age group. Defining generational birth years isn't
an exact science, but we'll use these generally accepted
definitions :

- Gen Z: 1997–2012[20]
- Millennials: 1981–1996[21]
- Gen X: 1965–1980[22]
- Baby Boomers: 1946–1964[23]
- Traditionalists: 1925–1945[24]

The percentages of each group in the workforce are
generally calculated as follows:

- Gen Z: 5 percent
- Millennials: 35 percent
- Gen X: 33 percent
- Baby Boomers: 25 percent
- Traditionalists: 2 percent[25]

Personal characteristics, job priorities, and preferred
methods of communication vary from group to group.
How a company communicates its mission and strategy to
each age group significantly impacts their individual job
performance and satisfaction. In general, today's workers
are increasingly seeking a work-life balance, purposeful
work, companies with social consciousness, flexible

schedules, and hybrid office-remote options. Employers need to be aware of and provide for these varied desires.

When today's millennials and Gen Z workers are feeling unsatisfied and unfulfilled, they might be vocal about it: they'll share their dissatisfaction on social media or workplace review sites such as Glassdoor. The flip side is if they feel they're fulfilling a greater purpose in their job and are proud of their company, they're equally likely to share their positive experience publicly.

The pandemic accelerated what's known as "The Great Resignation," a mass exodus from the workforce. According to US Department of Labor statistics, over 47 million workers voluntarily left their jobs in 2021, compared to over 36 million in 2020.[26] Millennials, the largest percentage of the current workforce, have been the fastest generation ever to quit. Nevertheless, they sometimes get a bad rap. They may not be working at 7:30 a.m. but they'll send emails at 11:00 p.m. They'll walk through brick walls if you treat them individually and ensure that their daily activities contribute to something larger than themselves and the company.

Another significant phenomenon affecting the US work landscape is "The Great Retirement" or "The Silver Tsunami." This refers to the large numbers of Baby

Boomers who are retiring. By some accounts, ten thousand people a day are reaching retirement age.

The departure of seniors leaves a talent vacuum. Baby Boomers are more likely to be senior leaders in an organization, making significant contributions. To retain them, "employers should provide them with specific goals and deadlines, put them in mentor roles, and offer coaching-style feedback."[27] This population generally prefers more personalized communication; an example would be phone calls (an approach less favored by millennials and Gen Zs) instead of emails and messaging.

Knowledge Sharing

We've repeated so many times that good communication was key to execution, that it won't come as a big surprise that knowledge sharing is also fundamental to give employees the right environment to perform.

Knowledge sharing does not necessarily involve complicated tools and systems. The apprenticeship model we discuss earlier is an effective way to make sure employees, especially new ones, build the skills they need to perform. More generally, a simple way of thinking about knowledge is to determine if knowledge resides in people or in processes. The apprenticeship model is well adapted to organizations where employees hold the knowledge; for example, a small boating equipment company we work with has manufacturing operators who have been in the company for decades and have built an unparalleled expertise to manufacture high-end gear using a range of materials (aluminum, titanium, various types of wood, plastics, carbon fiber) in small batches; this expertise is key for the company's customer intimacy strategy because it allows them to rapidly ideate and create new products for high-end customers. On the other end, it makes recruiting difficult because the required know-how is so unique.

Other manufacturing companies following an operational excellence strategy may build knowledge into documented standards and production processes; this approach makes sense when the goal is to minimize deviation from a set standard; it helps with recruiting, as the skillset of prospective employees is less critical—but training on how to operate the machines is, as is solid process management.

Regardless of the strategy, knowledge sharing is critical to build a learning organization able to identify and roll out good practices, remember customer preferences, and act on industry insights; maybe more importantly, it maximizes execution alignment when all employees operate with a level playing field when it comes to critical information about their jobs, the rest of the company, and the company's ecosystem of clients, suppliers, and partners.

Being intentional about knowledge management also sends a strong signal to current and prospective employees that you are serious about their own development: good knowledge sharing practices foster a culture of continuous learning and set the expectation for a growth mindset. It promotes employee engagement, which we saw earlier is so important, by giving employees opportunities to expand their knowledge and skills and contribute in ever-expanding, meaningful ways. It also makes good business sense at a time when it can be challenging to retain employees: the more knowledge is shared, the less risk there is that the departure of a skilled employee will disrupt operations.

Diversity at Work

We have mentioned several times the value of the platinum rule in making employees feel seen and appreciated. The platinum rule celebrates the uniqueness of every employee and the different skills they bring. In other words, it celebrates the diversity of thoughts and behaviors among employees; that diversity of thought brings tangible benefits:

- Diverse perspectives foster innovation and creativity. It does not mean that you will suddenly create radically new products as Apple would; it means your company is better able to solve problems and address new challenges in its daily operations.
- Especially in uncertain times, employees who can bring a different perspective than the mainstream can help make better decisions; they can pressure-test and challenge conventional wisdom and bring to light data or dimensions that the group overlooked.
- Even if specific industry verticals, clients are not all cut from the same cloth; a workforce that reflects whatever diversity exists among your customers will help you better understand and connect with the people who buy your products and services.

Here again, behavioral analytics can help you understand how much diversity exists on your leadership team and among your employees; it is in your best interest to have "balancers" (employees with a markedly different behavioral profile from the rest of the group) to regularly challenge the established thinking and make sure new and different perspectives are considered.

Human Capital

General Prescriptions

- If you aren't using behavioral analytics, it's a good time to start!
- Implement formal onboarding program for new employees (first 90 days are critical)
- Invest in your employees—it pays off in spades
- Platinum Rule vs. Golden Rule
- Embrace diversity

Fig 9.1. Prescriptions for Human Capital

CHAPTER 9

The fifth key, human capital, is the lifeblood of your organization. It is imperative to align your employees with the company's strategies and to set them up for success (Fig. 9.1).

In this chapter we discussed:

1. The right people need to be hired for the right roles to execute a company's unique customer value proposition and strategy. Psychometric assessments like the Predictive Index Behavioral Assessment can help to determine if a candidate has the right work-related traits for the role, alongside the right values, skills, and experience.

2. Learning and development initiatives build employee engagement; they must be tailored to individual employees' personal tendencies and the position's requirements to lead them in the way they need to be led.

3. A good onboarding has an outsized impact on retention.

4. Knowledge sharing is critical to continuously improve operations, align employees around shared practices, foster employee development, and maintain high engagement.

5. Diversity among your employees is essential to be more creative, to make better decisions, and to better relate to your own diverse clients and stakeholders.

> **ONE MORE THING**

An Additional Perspective on Human Capital

In an article in *Term Sheet*, a newsletter for PE and VC professionals, San Francisco–based Alpine Investments' CEO, Graham Weaver, shared his perspective on human capital. And that perspective happens to be the same as ours: the only priority of any leader is to hire and retain the best of the best for the job.

You may think your business is very different from the way private equity firms operate. It may be. But Weaver's proposition is universal: success depends on who you work with. If you have employees or contractors, your success depends on your people too.

Haven't we heard this from thousands of places in the pandemic years? Yes! However, Weaver's argument is not the "warm and fuzzy" type of those who suddenly discovered in the pandemic that workers were human beings that deserved respect and attention. Weaver's is an economic argument: your people will literally make or break your business.

We're glad to put the spotlight on Weaver because his experience is 100 percent aligned with our clients' journey to improve their strategy execution.

ONE MORE THING

The Line-of-Sight approach to measure the execution capabilities of an organization puts people in the center. Line-of-Sight's unique approach is that it relies on employees, managers, and executives' perception of these capabilities. It is all about the people; any strategic plan is worthless if it is not understood by employees in a way that shapes their behavior toward outcomes that drive economic performance.

And that understanding is still not enough. You need people who are well suited for their job so that their behavior translates into productive and effective actions and decisions.

In truth, we need more Graham Weavers. Our client work shows that human capital tends to be the most neglected dimension of strategy execution. Consider this:

When Line-of-Sight surveyed 150-plus executives about the execution capabilities of their organizations in late 2020, CEOs nearly universally rated their human capital capabilities the lowest. It does not mean they gave their employees poor scores; it means their organizations did not have in place the right tools and mindset to do what Weaver says should be

(ONE MORE THING)

a leader's first and only priority: hire and retain the best for the job.

A diagnostic solution like Line-of-Sight is invaluable to show leaders where their gaps and risks are. And human capital risks are big—just look around you and you'll see businesses disrupted by their leaders' inability to attract and retain employees, whether they are your local eatery, a global airline, or a specialty manufacturer.

In our Line-of-Sight practice, we provide every organization with simple, confidence-inspiring analytics and solutions that build their internal alignment—and get things across the finish line. Just like Weaver, human capital is our priority to build and retain this alignment.

Your Organization's Health Index
Evaluation: People (Human Capital)

Use this rating scale to assess the execution capabilities of your organization in the table below:

A: Aligned (5 points)   M: Misaligned (-1 point)
S: Somewhat Aligned (2 points) N: Not Sure (0 points)

Index	People (Human Capital) Health Assessment Criteria	Your Assessment (A, S, M, N)	Your Score (5, 2, -1, 0 point)
HC1	We receive training that enables us to perform activities that contribute to the effective execution of our company strategy.		
HC2	We continuously share knowledge and ideas that help create unique customer value and contribute to our company strategy.		
HC3	Our company attracts and retains employees with the talent and skills needed to create competitive advantage.		

Total Score _____

From a People standpoint, the health of your organization is as follows:

- If your total score is 7 or less, your organization is not feeling well.

- If your score is between 7 and 12, your organization is going about its day but is not able to run a sprint without feeling depleted.
- If your score is 12 or above, your organization is very fit. It can tackle any challenge that the world throws at it.

People Prescriptions If Your Health Score Is 12 or Below

Align Talent Strategy with Business Strategy

At the highest level, the talent strategy should be aligned with the company's market discipline. This means that the business strategy should inform:

- What type of behaviors the company wants and needs to incentivize, i.e. broadly defined as which culture the company wants to foster.
- What type of leadership team will be most effective to execute the strategy.
- What type of employees and managers need to be hired and developed internally.
- What type of training is necessary to shape the attitudes and aptitudes that will help execute the strategy.

All talent-related decisions and activities should be informed by the market discipline and by the strategy of the organization.

Use Objective Data

Decisions related to human capital should be made with the same rigor and objectivity as is used in other functions like finance and manufacturing. If it does not already, the company should use behavioral analytics to:

- Hire employees
- Coach and develop employees and managers
- Help the executive team operate at its peak performance.

Foster Awareness of Self and Others

Behavioral analytics should be used to build and maintain awareness of self and others across the organization as a lever for personal and team effectiveness, to:

- Ensure that every employee has access to behavioral data about themselves and their colleagues, so as to inform every interaction.
- Have senior executives lead by example by frequently referring to their own behavioral patterns and showing interest and knowledge about others.
- Train managers to use behavioral data to be effective leaders at all levels of the organization and to apply the "platinum rule" in the hiring, management, and development of their team members.

Ensure Employee and Job Fit

Right people, right role—the basic condition for successful execution
is to have the right talent, i.e. making sure employees are well-suited
for their job, both in aptitude (technical skills) and attitude (behavior).
The latter cannot be assessed reliably unless you use behavioral
analytics tools such as the Predictive Index to:

- Define job requirements
- Assess candidates against these requirements
- Coach employees to continuously optimize their performance
  and personal fulfillment

Train for Success

Develop training programs that are:

- Directly aligned with the strategic goals
- Able to address the execution gaps highlighted in the
  Organizational Scan
- Consistent with the behavioral makeup of employees, so that
  training and coaching address individual development oppor-
  tunities to maximize job fit

Bolster Knowledge Sharing

- Build multiple channels to share information, such as:
  - ▸ Bulletin boards
  - ▸ Emails
  - ▸ Newsletter

- ▸ Slack, or other collaboration apps
- ▸ Formal knowledge-sharing sessions
- ▸ Dedicated agenda item on cross-functional team meetings
- Make sure the executive team leads by example by sharing extensively from the top, especially about the strategy and performance of the company.
- Make sure the executive team maintains a psychologically safe culture that encourages all employees to share data and information without the fear of being judged or criticized.
- Reassess incentives and performance management systems to prevent knowledge hoarding and self-centered behaviors; generally, develop incentives that reward collaboration.
- Organize knowledge sharing:
  - ▸ Make an individual and team accountable for knowledge management
  - ▸ Invest in simple tools to store, retrieve, and share knowledge and make communication and collaboration easy (e.g. Slack, Google).

CHAPTER 10

Determining Your Organization's Health Index: How Well Are You Executing?

In this section, you can evaluate the overall execution capabilities of your own organization, by aggregating your scores from the previous chapters.

Report in the table below the scores you've assigned to your organization capabilities in each of the 5 KSEs:

- Strategic Understanding (see your report card on page 90)
- Leadership (see your report card on page 110)
- Balanced Metrics (see your report card on page 135)
- Activities & Structure (see your report card on page 156)
- Human Capital (see your report card on page 180)

Key to Strategic Execution	Your Score (in points)
Strategic Understanding of	
Leadership	
Balanced Metrics	
Activities & Structure	
Human Capital	
Overall Index	

- **If your overall health index is 50 or less,** your organization is not feeling well.
- **If your overall health index is between 51 and 85,** your organization is going about its day but is not able to run a sprint without feeling depleted.
- **If your overall health index is 86 or above,** your organization is very fit. It can tackle any challenge that the world throws at it.

How Do You Compare to Other Leaders?

You might wonder how your scores compare with other organizations. In 2021 we ran a survey to evaluate how well organizations execute, across a range of industries and company sizes. To make it an apple-to-apple comparison, we'll only focus on the self-reported scores we gathered in that survey; that way you can benchmark your scores against the scores that other business leaders assigned to their own organization. We can do this because we polled about 150 CEOs and they told us about the health of their organization across the five KSEs.

Our survey showed a typical "execution curve" that is surprisingly consistent across companies (Fig. 10.1).

On average, leaders rank the execution capabilities of their organization highest for Strategic Understanding,

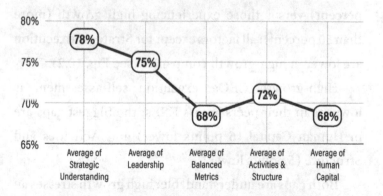

Fig. 10.1. The Execution Curve – Average KSE scores

and lowest for Balanced Metrics and Human Capital. In other words, CEOs rate their execution performance better on the "front office"—developing the strategy and being effective stewards of the strategy by clearly and broadly articulating it to the organization, and relatively weaker on the "back office"—setting up and operating the reporting, structure, and talent optimization practices that bring the strategy to fruition.

Growing Too Fast Will Cost You

We found out that growth and execution health are related. It is always tricky to determine causality, but the scores we've seen in our survey suggest that high growth can negatively impact your ability to execute, which stands to reason. This is clear when we compare KSE scores for companies experiencing moderate growth (5 to 50 percent) versus those experiencing high growth (more than 50 percent): all factors except for Strategic Execution are lower in high-growth companies (see Fig. 10.2).

High-growth CEOs' execution self-assessment is lower than their peers across KSEs; the biggest gaps are in Human Capital (6 points lower) and Activities and Structure (5 points lower).

Both gaps are understandable: high growth stresses an organization's ability to hire in large volumes, to properly

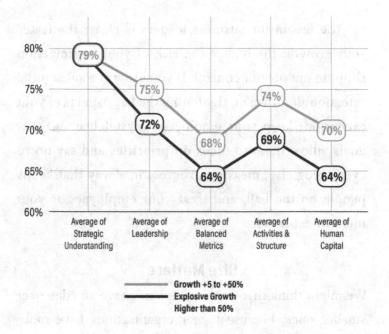

Fig. 10.2. Growth impacts execution – KSE scores by company growth rate

onboard and train new employees, to develop managers to help them lead larger teams, and to deliberately shape a positive culture.

The gap in Activities and Structure is even less surprising: when growth is fast, employees are challenged to stay focused on priorities; reporting lags behind operations, leaving employees flying blind without accurate or timely data to confirm that they are executing the most critical areas.

The lesson for business leaders is clear: the faster your growth, the higher the risk of your organization slipping out of your control. If you grow at a substantial rate, double-down on tightening the key aspects of your execution: keep your employees crystalclear on your goals, allow them to focus on priorities and say no to everything else, measure progress in a way that keeps people on the ball, and treat your employees as your most valuable asset.

Size Matters

We might think that larger companies have an edge over smaller ones, because bigger organizations have more resources to dedicate to things like strategic planning, dashboards, and employee training. To confirm this assumption, we reviewed the data to see whether large companies (of more than five hundred employees) had any execution advantage compared to small-to-midsize companies.

The results are counterintuitive: the data actually suggests the opposite is happening. CEOs of mid-sized companies (150 to 500 employees) rate their own execution performance slightly higher than CEOs of small companies (less than 150 employees), and significantly higher than large companies (see Fig. 10.3).

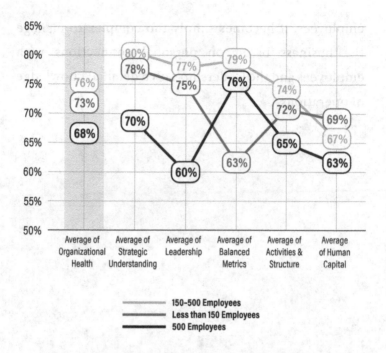

150–500 Employees
Less than 150 Employees
500 Employees

Fig. 10.3. Organizational KSE scores by company size

The edge that mid-size companies have over their smaller peers is admittedly small: their aggregate Organization Health Index is only higher by 3 points, at 76 versus 73, and data suggests that their index is only higher because of a large difference in balanced metrics in favor of mid-size companies.

It may be explained by the fact that size itself often compels companies to invest into more robust reporting systems, payroll and HRIS, and ERP; beyond 150 employees, it becomes simply too complex to manage the business based on personal connections with employees and the leadership's own detailed knowledge of operations.

Should We Continue the Conversation?

You are now armed with effective tools tailored for small- and medium-sized businesses and are able to generate significant enhancements of your execution capabilities and results. It is our sincere hope that your next decisions will incorporate some of the practices you've learned here.

There are more resources at your disposal:

Our Website

www.thelineofsight.com gives you access to more tools and tips to improve your organizational health. On our website, you'll find the following:

- Execution Health self-assessment
- Tools to evaluate the execution capabilities of your company, and to compare your score with your team and your employees
- Case studies showing how other companies decided to improve their performance by executing better
- Access to Line-of-Sight certified consultants near you

Keynotes and Presentations

Bring the authors of this book, Robert Courser and Olivier Aries, to engage your organization in thinking differently about execution.

Line–of–Sight Consultants

If you are determined to execute better and eliminate the execution tax that drains your margin and your energy, if you are facing an immediate execution issue, or if you prefer to have a partner by your side as you move forward with Line-of-Sight practices, you can engage one of our

Line-of-Sight expert consultants to baseline your organization and help you build your capabilities toward execution excellence.

The Line–of–Sight Approach

This is a process that typically unfolds over twelve months (see Fig. 11.1).

Our assessment tools, the Line-of-Sight Enterprise Survey and the Line-of-Sight Pulse Checks, are used to assess your organization's baseline of readiness and ability to execute on the strategy. Pulse Checks are used to get real-time data on progress for areas of improvement.

Once the initial survey has helped develop the execution baseline (i.e. how well your organization is executing right now), the most critical milestone is the two-day Strategy Facilitation Briefing. This session takes place

Fig. 11.1. How Line-of-Sight gets to execution excellence

with your leadership team. It will equip your team with the knowledge and skills to "reset the clock" on execution and start managing execution with accuracy and precision.

The briefing covers:

- Clarifying Mission, Vision, and Strategic Intent
- Reviewing your baseline scores for:
  - ▸ Market Discipline
  - ▸ Strategic Understanding
  - ▸ Leadership
  - ▸ Balanced Metrics
  - ▸ Activities & Structure
  - ▸ Human Capital
- Developing action plans for each KSE, with accountabilities

After the briefing has taken place, it is all about practice and repetition. Quarterly plan reviews help your team stay on course, using Line-of-Sight as an accountability tool, and measure the impact of action plans and corrective measures. These sessions bring discipline and an outside-in, factual perspective needed to implement the health improvement actions planned during the strategic briefing. Each session includes a progress assessment, learnings from execution in the period, adjustments to the improvement plans, and fact-based reviews by your executive team to maintain their alignment and focus on execution gaps. Each session concludes with a documented plan and accountabilities for the next quarter.

Finally, with monthly check-ins we assist you in pinpointing areas of misalignment so you can take action, identify priorities each month, and put solutions in place based on monthly progress reports.

What Does Execution Excellence Look Like? A Client Case Study of the Line-of-Sight Methodology

How does it feel to use the Line-of-Sight approach to execute better?

To give you a sense of the power of execution analytics, we will discuss here the data, insights, and performance improvements of an actual Line-of-Sight client—a manufacturing company developing high-end recreational vehicles with a six- to seven-figure price tag.

The starting point was the realization by senior executives that the company seemed to be unable to exceed a particular production threshold. Year in, year out, the same number of vehicles came out the door despite a growing market and robust demand. In fact, that demand was allowing the company to post modest revenue growth numbers through price increases, but nowhere near the magnitude increase the leadership wanted. Production was marginally increasing year-over-year, but it seemed due more to hard work and personal initiative from employees than from a deliberate, concerted plan. It was clear that what had taken them to this point was not what they needed to grow beyond their production bottleneck.

The Line-of-Sight-based improvement program started by inviting every employee, from frontline associates to the senior leadership team, to take the Line-of-Sight survey. The senior leadership team (SLT) then met for two days for a strategy facilitation meeting, during which every aspect of their execution was picked apart and reviewed to identify opportunities to improve their strategic focus and their operations.

We will highlight here the key elements of this diagnostic, and the key recommendations that came out of

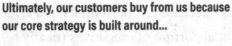

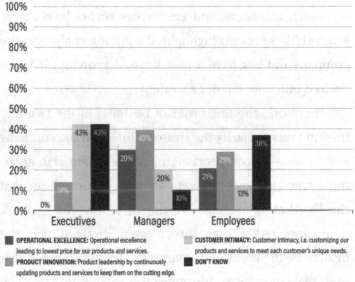

Fig. A.1. Why do customers buy from us?

it. The visuals come from the standard Execution Health Assessment survey.

The first challenge was that the SLT was not sure why their customers were buying from them (Fig. A.1).

The table shows how different stakeholders in the company had a different understanding of what clients valued in the company: senior leaders thought it was customer intimacy and the ability to customize their vehicle; managers thought it was because the product was innovative or perhaps because it represented good value; worse yet, a substantial portion of executives (nearly half of them), managers, and employees across levels were unsure! These results highlighted a glaring challenge: the company did not have a plan beyond growing. It had a desired outcome but not a strategy.

Therefore, the first order of business in the two-day meeting was to clarify the strategic intent of the company and its basis for competition; it became essential to determine who the customer actually was. It turned out that the distribution model, by relying on a powerful network of dealers rather than direct sales, dictated that the dealers be the focus on the strategy. The SLT agreed that their real competitive advantage was their ability to make their product easily customizable by dealers, which in turn were using the product's versatile design to generate substantial revenues by personalizing the product for their end customers and upselling their own equipment. In many ways, the product was a customizable platform, and this was an essential asset for the dealers.

The company was also very effective at customizing the delivery to each dealer's preferences, since some preferred the vehicle to be turn-key ready for customer personalization, while others did delivery preparation themselves.

The next step of the diagnostic was to assess how well the company strategy was understood by employees, and how well it informed their daily work. In many companies, the strategy is reasonably well documented by the leadership, but breaks down when it comes to sharing it with employees.

The SLT acknowledged that employees were most likely not aligned with the strategy; interestingly enough, however, managers and employees figured that things were pretty clear (see Fig. A.2). We see this paradox in similar situations: "strategic vacuum" (there is no

Measures individual understanding of the company's strategy.

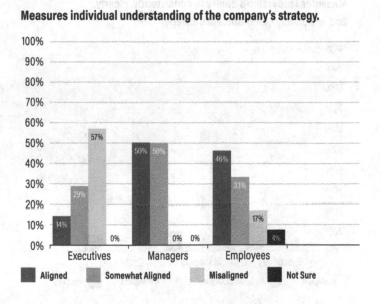

Fig. A.2. Individual understanding of the strategy

real strategy) forces employees to guess what they are supposed to be doing and come up with a strategic rationale on their own to give meaning to their daily job. In this case, the issue was compounded by the fact that few employees had an appreciation for how high-end and customizable the product was; indeed, the company was located in a rural area without any industrial tradition for the type of product that it built; therefore, the workforce lacked the deep manufacturing experience and points of comparison to appreciate the entire strategic picture. Up

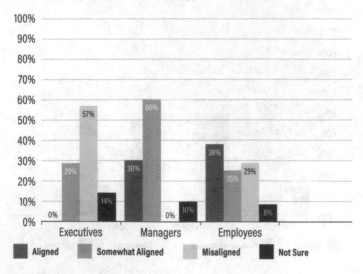

Measures leadership's ability to consistently, clearly, and actionably communicate strategy.

Fig. A.3. Communication of the strategy by leadership

to this point, the leadership had not provided that broader exposition and education to employees either. That point was made clear when looking at strategy communication (Fig. A.3).

The SLT acknowledged their own shortcomings in terms of strategy communication, and employees saw as much—everyone saw what they wanted to see. Interestingly, managers had a more positive view of strategy communication, and this is because, faced with the need to provide clear and actionable directions to their teams as the only stated goal was to grow production, they had to make their own assumptions about the company strategy, and therefore considered the lack of strategic guidance from the top with more leniency.

The situation was marginally better for metrics, but leaders and managers had a rosier view of the situation than employees. The only number that mattered to the top was the number of units produced by production line by week, but the survey made clear it was not enough for employees to operate in an environment with clear direction and the ability to self-inspect and self-correct (Fig. A.4).

Managers turned out to be adept at organically plugging another hole in the company's execution: budgeting (see Fig. A.5).

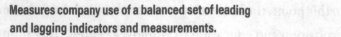

Measures company use of a balanced set of leading and lagging indicators and measurements.

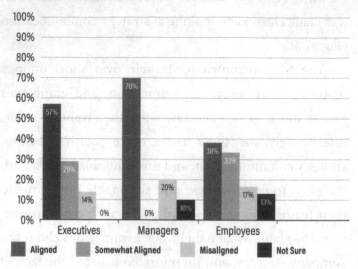

Fig. A.4. Use of balanced metrics

The company had been able to operate without a clear strategy for a long period of time because it had a decentralized structure: each department had a P&L-like budget and relative control over its use. As a result, managers once again felt comfortable that budgets aligned with what they thought the strategy was, even though the SLT themselves recognized that the lack of a clear strategy was a challenge for budgeting.

The primary reason why the company struggled to grow was the lack of focus of employees (Fig. A.6). When

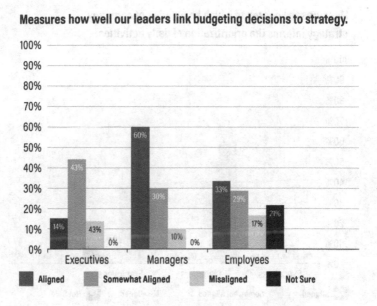

Measures how well our leaders link budgeting decisions to strategy.

Fig. A.5. Linking budgeting decisions to strategy

asked how much strategic direction informed the prioritization of their daily tasks, we see confusion: 38 percent thought they were clear, 38 percent thought they were somewhat clear, nearly 20 percent felt misaligned, and nearly 10 percent didn't really know. No wonder the company struggled to organize its resources around a small number of well-communicated priorities.

The final key challenge was the lack of support employees were receiving (Fig. A.7). Training was acknowledged to be insufficient and/or not relevant enough to expand employees skills.

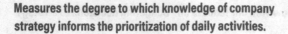

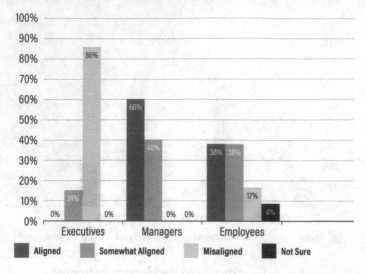

Fig. A.6. Link between strategy and daily activities

Once the diagnosis was on the table, the rest of the SLT working sessions were focused on developing action plans to address the execution gaps. The recommendations were fundamentally simple. First, we helped the SLT to revisit and polish their mission and vision; the strategic intent was revised to enhance the company's focus on customer intimacy, i.e. the ability to customize products to meet the differentiated needs of their dealers.

The company leaders, equipped with this clarified focus, went on a "roadshow" to make sure the newly

Measures how well training and development efforts are employed to enable strategy-enhancing performance and effective execution.

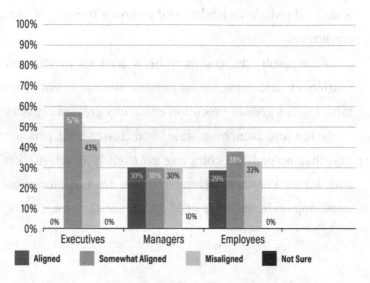

Fig. A.7. Alignment of employee training & development with strategy and execution

revised strategy was understood by every employee. One of the most remarkable (and fun) events was a "friends and family" show that re-introduced the workforce (and their families) to the product; it was an opportunity for all of them to really appreciate the value and craftsmanship of the finished product and see it through the eyes of their customers. It turned out to be a pivotal moment to build collective pride and for each employee to see their role in the larger whole of the company.

That was not all: key production processes were also documented, including the use of videos to standardize work and reduce variability and improve training of new employees.

As a result, the company blew past its production bottleneck and grew by 40 percent within twenty-four months. The greater execution efficiency created capacity to design and launch an additional, faster-built product line that helped the company go slightly down-market with larger volumes without straying from its focus on satisfying their customer need for personalization.

Robert Courser's Nine Principles
for Execution Excellence

The Founder's Trap

An entrepreneurial leader's inability to adapt to changing circumstances. It can lead to a failure to scale the company based on their initial vision. Recognize when you are caught in it.

Engagement Through Purpose

A shared sense of purpose and contribution throughout all levels of an organization that leads to both employee and company success. Employees are engaged when they understand that what they do every day matters and feel that their work is purposeful.

Valuing Employees

Valuing your workers and their activities leads to value for your customer, and ultimately, the company.

Increasing Engagement

To reach disengaged workers and increase their commitment, persistence in over-communicating the company's vision, mission, and strategic intent is key. Repetition and reinforcement of the message can capture employees' attention and lead to a sense of pride in their work, resulting in a competitive advantage for the business.

Work *on* the Business Instead of *in* the Business

Assessing your organization's strengths and weaknesses through self-inspection can lead to increased self-awareness and opportunities for self-correction.

Strategy First, Organizational Structure Next

A company needs to know its vision *before* determining what organizational structure will help realize it and hiring new employees.

Deliberate Strategy

A successful business strategy requires you to define your unique value proposition, value chain, and capabilities to deliver on your unique promise to customers. Leaders must place high importance on ensuring that all employees understand the business's strategy.

Effective Leadership

Effective leaders know how to 1) build credibility, 2) communicate in a sustained and consistent manner, and

3) lead change by adapting its pace and approach to the behavioral make-up of their employees.

Balanced Metrics

Ask yourself what you intend to learn by measuring. If you learn what you intended to, will you do anything differently? If the answer is yes, measure away. But if the answer is no, it's not worth it.

Acknowledgments

I cannot begin to truly express my thanks and gratitude for the thought leadership, mentorship, and continued support in my life of the following individuals:

Paul Gille, friend, strategy guru, and mentor;

Dick Singer, directly responsible for helping me transition from executive chef to executive;

Charlie Garcia for starting me down the path of execution and challenging me to think differently;

Charles Gounaris, who gave me the most practical grasp of strategy and execution;

Brian Raduenz for running one of the coolest companies;

My co author Olivier Aries for the drive and gumption to push me across the finish line;

Lisa Johnson for making sure nothing falls through the cracks.

Kat Daley for providing invaluable feedback on this book manuscript.

To the founding Line-of-Sight implementers, Chris and Ana Quinn, Brandon and Lisa Kinsey, Eric and Alina Kish, Dave and Christine Nast, John Broer and Sara Best, Shawna and Robin Reed, Zach Schaefer, Trent Lee, Sergiu Simmel, and Alexander Portnoy: thank you for your determination and continued support.

To Gene Jones and Robert Sullivan: thank you for your continued support and guidance.

To Rabih Shanshiry, Matt Poepsel, Daniel Muzquiz, Mike Zani, and the entire team at the Predictive Index: thank you for your support as we built our practice over the years. To Nancy Martini, who straddles the worlds of the Predictive Index and Line of Sight: thank you for your vision.

And to Joseph Nicholson, my most loyal lieutenant: your dedication, support, and friendship mean the world to me.

Notes

1 Ron Carucci, "Executives Fail to Execute Strategy Because They're Too Internally Focused", *Harvard Business Review*, November 13, 2017, https://hbr.org/2017/11/executives-fail-to-execute-strategy-because-theyre-too-internally-focused.

2 Richard Fry, "Millennials Are the Largest Generation in the U.S. Labor Force," *Pew Research Center*, April 11, 2018, https://www.pewresearch.org/short-reads/2018/04/11/millennials-largest-generation-us-labor-force/.

3 Valerie Bolden-Barrett, "Millennials Seek Meaning at Work--and Employers Can Help," *HR Dive*, October 30, 2019, https://www.hrdive.com/news/millennials-seek-meaning-at-work-and-employers-can-help/566118/.

4 "Engaging and Empowering Millennials," *PWC*, accessed September 21, 2023,https://www.pwc.com/gx/en/hr-management-services/publications/assets/pwc-engaging-and-empowering-millennials.pdf.

5 "Apple Research and Development Expenses 2010-2023," *Macrotrends*, https://www.macrotrends.net/stocks/charts/AAPL/apple/research-development-expenses.

6 Mihir Mysore, Aditya Sanghvi, Navjot Singh, and Bob Sternfels, "Speed and Resilience: Five Priorities for the Next Five Months", *McKinsey& Company*, March 29, 2021, https://www.mckinsey.com/capabilities/people-and-organizational-performance/our-insights/speed-and-resilience-five-priorities-for-the-next-five-months.

7 "Engaging and Empowering Millennials."

8 Robert S. Kaplan and David P. Norton, "The Office of Strategy Management," *Harvard Business Review*, October 2005, https://hbr.org/2005/10/the-office-of-strategy-management.

9 Katie Lange, "The Challenge Coin Tradition: Do You Know How It Started?," *US Department of Defense*, DOD News, October 8, 2017, https://www.defense.gov/News/Inside-DOD/Blog/Article/2567302/the-challenge-coin-tradition-do-you-know-how-it-started.

10 R. Scott Russell, "Gallup Reports Historic Drop in Employee Engagement Following Record Rise," *C. A. Short*, July 31, 2020, https://www.cashort.com/blog/gallup-reports-historic-drop-in-employee-engagement-following-record-rise.

11 Jim Harter, "U.S. Employee Engagement Slump Continues," *Gallup: Workplace*, April 25, 2022, https://www.gallup.com/workplace/391922/employee-engagement-slump-continues.aspx.

12 Dana Rousmaniere, "Prioritize the Business Relationships that Matter Most," *Harvard Business Review*, April 27, 2016, https://hbr.org/tip/2016/04/prioritize-the-business-relationships-that-matter-most.

13 Bruce Lee, *Tao of Jeet Kune Do*, (Valencia, CA: Ohara Publications, 1975).

14 Daniel Eisenberg and Deidre Paknad, "Building a 'Digital Operating Rhythm' with OKR Software," May 17, 2022, in *Mckinsey on Start-ups*, podcast, MP3 audio, https://www.mckinsey.com/industries/technology-media-and-telecommunications/our-insights/building-a-digital-operating-rhythm-with-okr-software.

15 Eisenberg and Paknad, "Building a 'Digital Operating Rhythm.'"

16 Eisenberg and Paknad, "Building a 'Digital Operating Rhythm.'"

17 "The Human Capital Project: Frequently Asked Questions," Human Capitol Project, The World Bank, updated October 03, 2022, https://www.worldbank.org/en/publication/human-capital/brief/the-human-capital-project-frequently-asked-questions.

18 Greg Barnett, "How to Understand Different Types of Employee Behavior in the Workplace," *People Management* (blog), *The Predictive Index*, https://www.predictiveindex.com/blog/the-four-key-factors-that-determine-workplace-behavior/#the-four-drives-that-determine-workplace-behavior.

19 John Hunter, "Why do you hire dead wood? Or why do you hire live wood and kill it?" *The Deming Institute Blog* (blog), *The Deming Institute*, August 06, 2015, https://deming.org/why-do-you-hire-dead-wood-or-why-do-you-hire-live-wood-and-kill-it/.

20 Alison Eldridge, "Generation Z: demographic group," in *Encyclopedia Britannica*, updated June 21, 2023, https://www.britannica.com/topic/Generation-Z

21 Alicja Zelazko, "millennial: demographic group," in *Encyclopedia Britannica*, updated June 29, 2023, https://www.britannica.com/topic/millennial

22 Amy McKenna, "Generation X: demographic group," in *Encyclopedia Britannica*, updated June 29, 2023, https://www.britannica.com/topic/Generation-X

23 Philip Bump, "baby boomers: American demographic group," in *Encyclopedia*

Britannica, updated June 29, 2023, https://www.britannica.com/topic/baby-boomers

24 Jeff Wallenfeldt, "Silent Generation: demographic group," in *Encyclopedia Britannica*, updated June 29, 2023, https://www.britannica.com/topic/Silent-Generation

25 "Generational Differences in the Workplace," Perdue Global, accessed May 23, 2023, https://www.purdueglobal.edu/education-partnerships/generational-workforce-differences-infographic/.

26 Joseph Fuller and William Kerr, "The Great Resignation Didn't Start with the Pandemic," *Harvard Business Review*, March 23, 2022, https://hbr.org/2022/03/the-great-resignation-didnt-start-with-the-pandemic.

27 Melna Jones, "Generational Differences in the Workplace," LinkedIn, July 5, 2022, https://www.linkedin.com/pulse/generational-differences-workplace-melna-jones-pcc-pmp/.